American Farmers
and
The Rise of Agribusiness

Seeds of Struggle

American Farmers
and
The Rise of Agribusiness

Seeds of Struggle

Advisory Editors

Dan C. McCurry
Richard E. Rubenstein

THE PLUNGER
A TALE OF THE WHEAT PIT

EDWARD JEROME DIES

ARNO PRESS

A New York Times Company

New York — 1975

Reprint Edition 1975 by Arno Press Inc.

Reprinted from a copy in
The Pennsylvania State Library

AMERICAN FARMERS AND THE RISE OF AGRIBUSINESS:
Seeds of Struggle
ISBN for complete set: 0-405-06760-7
See last pages of this volume for titles.

Manufactured in the United States of America

◄►

Library of Congress Cataloging in Publication Data

Dies, Edward Jerome, 1891-
     The plunger, a tale of the wheat pit.

     (American farmers and the rise of agribusiness)
     Reprint of the 1929 ed. published by Covici-Friede,
New York.
     1. Hutchinson, Benjamin P., 1828-1899. 2. Grain
trade--Chicago. 3. Chicago. Board of Trade. I. Ti-
tle. II. Series.
HG6047.G8D47 1975   813'.5'2   74-30627
ISBN 0-405-06789-5

THE PLUNGER

The Pit—1928
"*The dark pile of quaint architecture blocking the foot of
La Salle Street seems ever in danger of being swallowed up
in a jungle of skyscrapers.*"

EDWARD JEROME DIES

THE PLUNGER
A TALE OF THE WHEAT PIT

PUBLISHED IN NEW YORK
BY COVICI-FRIEDE
1929

TYPOGRAPHY BY S. A. JACOBS
PRINTED IN THE UNITED STATES OF AMERICA
BY STRATFORD PRESS, NEW YORK

Contents

"Life is a song sung by an idiot, dancing down the wind."
                                                EURIPIDES.

I

Ghosts of Memory

THE dim roar of the Pit was like the muffled note of a distant organ.

Up in the tower, high above the crowd of frantic traders, a weary old man sat alone, with eyes closed and head tipped forward as if in sleep. His long legs were stretched out at full length, and his great arms dangled to the floor in utter abandon.

The hushed, whimsical drone of the Pit had been soothing, like an autumn wind blowing old memories through moonlit, tossing trees. But now and then it would change, with the suddenness of a wind, and take on a deeper and drearier tone. Once it rose like the roar of a blast as it rumbled through the tower. The old man sat upright and listened intently. In another moment the roar had drifted off into a shivery choral wail that gave a feeling of melancholy. He slumped deeper into his chair, and waited. At length a gong sounded, heralding the close of the day's trading. The tumult and clamor ended abruptly. In another hour the silence was like that of a cathedral.

An afternoon sun had slipped down the western wall, and stars glittered in the sky before Old Hutch stirred from his reverie. Slowly he arose and groped his way through the darkness to a little door opening upon a flight of narrow spiral stairs that ran from top to bottom of the structure.

He descended carefully, laboriously, picking his steps with infinite pains, feeling along the wall with one hand and with the other clutching a volume of his beloved Shakespeare. At each landing he would stop for a moment, breathe deeply, and then continue on his way, finally coming out upon the low-slung balcony just over the Wheat Pit.

Here he dropped upon a seat, leaned heavily against the railing, and stared down into the yawning Pit. Across the broad trading floor shadows from street lights and passing vehicles danced about crazily, taking on grotesque shapes, racing back and forth and up and down with the aimless capers of a nightmare.

Memories crowded his mind—blasted hopes, defeat, victories, high adventure. In his fancy he called up the ghosts of long dead plungers, former cronies who,

"A narrow beam of yellow light grew into a shower and sunshine, and the big trading hall became a glowing mass of Pompeian red and gold."

like himself, had tasted Pit life; comets that had flashed across the speculative skies.

Like the shifting shadows of a dream he saw them, gray and dim, gathered in the trading ring below, struggling back and forth, trying with agonizing efforts to make themselves heard above the tumult. He saw arms swinging wildly and nimble fingers writing prices in the air. He fancied each of the vague misty figures was at that very moment meeting the great crisis of his life. In some he thought he saw the ghastly pallor of ruin; in others the hot fever of determination. With a feeling of life's hopelessness he recalled the blunders of each, the fatal slips that had brought disaster. The very thought sickened, and thrusting the memories from his mind he muttered in a tone of irony:

"Failures. Ghosts. All ghosts!"

Then he slept. . . .

A narrow beam of yellow light against a satin surface of brownish mahogany gradually widened and grew into a shower of sunshine that flooded the balcony. It poured through those stained glass windows that rival famous medieval compositions, and the big trading hall gradually became a glowing mass of Pompeian red and gold.

An attendant, making his early morning round to see

that all was in readiness for the day, came upon the old man in the balcony. For a long moment he stood still, a quizzical expression on his face. Then he drew nearer and with a gentle hand touched him upon the shoulder.

"Why, Mr. Hutchinson," he said, "what in the world are you doing here so early?"

The quick mind of Old Hutch caught up the words, and he replied:

"Reading, son; only reading. It is an inspiration to sit here in the early morning sunlight and read and dream and think. Words seem to strike more deeply, and their meaning lights up the dark corners of the mind."

"Yet today," he added with a deep sigh, "words and verse and sunlight cannot nurse me back to happiness. Nothing shall ever bring me back. My day is done; my hope is dead."

"Listen to this," he continued, opening the thumb-worn volume:

" 'Freeze, freeze, thou bitter sky,
    Thou dost not bite so nigh
      As benefits forgot:
    Though thou the waters warp,
    Thy sting is not so sharp
      As friend remember'd not.' "

The volume closed with a snap. The old man tucked it under his arm, walked down to the main floor, bade the attendent farewell, and stepped out into the morning sunshine. He likewise stepped out of the lives of his friends and associates, and largely out of the mind of the public.

It was the passing of Old Hutch. A Wheat King had lost his throne. . . .

Long ago the star of Wheat Pit freedom began paling under the powerful lens of government control. What were once deemed the sacred trade secrets of the big plunger are now an open book—a daily record that may be viewed by a staff of government officials with power to inquire into the precise position of each trader. And behind these officers stands an inflexible law preventing misuse of the marketing machinery for private gain.

So the days of Pit romance are dead; the old time plunger, who lashed markets into submission and bent them to his will, has slowly faded into obscurity. Only the memory of his intrepid exploits remains.

No one so typified the tumultuous period as did Old Hutch. For he was the pivotal point in a mad panorama, whirling and fantastic, that stretched across two decades of Wheat Pit history and touched them into color. Always the dreamer and philosopher, his stroke was yet powerful, and his aim true and deadly.

Against a background of confusion and stress, a strained and heaving commerce plunging toward a new dawn, this dark, mysterious figure glides back and forth across the Pit, fighting, struggling, scheming, cursing, and singing. He sang loudest when they expected him to weep, and in the full tide of his own glory, he sat apart and grieved at the woes of a wicked world.

He was roundly hated and bitterly denounced. In periods of unpopularity there were those dismal commentators who likened him to the Russian Grand Dukes who flogged moujiks for daring to complain of illness; and to Cossacks who shot down the assembled people who had the temerity to present a petition. When he was seated safely and happily upon his throne, and his word was law to the Wheat Pit, his critics likened him to *Le Roi Soleil*, the magnificent old rascal who lounged through the barbaric splendors of Versailles, played with wantons of Trianon, and said, "The State? I am the State!" For Old Hutch was the Wheat Pit.

At their jibes he only laughed, tightened his lines, and rushed on toward what he believed with an unflagging faith to be his golden destiny.

If he was the object of a withering hatred, the love

and affection heaped upon him was perhaps of like intensity. For had he not always tempered justice with mercy? It was he who first offered succor to the very Pit victims whom he had cuffed and mauled and pounded into submission. Even his most annoying enemies, if indeed he found them annoying, might confess their wrongdoings, gain absolution, and find food, drink, and shelter at his lively fireside.

But in the fever of a campaign he neither asked nor gave quarter. He seemed to know no fear, brushed aside doubt and misgiving, and flayed his army of antagonists with stinging words of disdain that goaded them on to greater battle. Fighting the crowd alone, matching his craft and judgment against overwhelming odds, he became a furious giant of strength, powerful and inexhaustible. On and on he would plunge with his millions, while the outlines of the weather map swung about like garments on a windy clothes line. He was impervious to dangers that normally sway the course of markets and dash the unwary plunger to his doom. He solemnly believed himself the fated master of the Wheat Pit and all that it meant to commerce and society.

When at last he did close his iron hand around much of the bread supply of the world, and the public gasped in amazement, he too showed unfeigned surprise—surprise that a thankless nation should have failed to visualize the coming spectacle, surprise that his act was not deemed one of genuine public good, at least for the producer. And later on, when a hero-worshipping public clapped upon him the title of "Napoleon of Wheat," he turned a wry smile to his admirers and quoted verse on the emptiness of public praise. That was Old Hutch.

But there was no evidence then or later to indicate that the title was really distasteful. On the contrary, there were those who steadfastly believed that Old Hutch dreamed of world power; they pointed to his feverish study of the great conquerors, his minute analyses of food supplies the world over, his subtle toying with foreign markets during the long years of partial mastery over American grain channels. Some critics said that just as Napoleon had read too much Roman history to be blinded to the vision of world rulership, so had Old Hutch steeped himself too thoroughly in the exploits of both military and economic conquerors. They hotly asserted that he had visions of a power so tremendous as to rock the financial structure, a power that might rise to a virtual dictatorship in the matter of foodstuffs, if only for a brief, dramatic period.

So wagged the tongue of gossip.

It is true, however, that on at least two occasions the "Napoleon of Wheat" had it within his means to bring down a money panic in which a large number of firms could have been swept to ruin. No other master of the Wheat Pit, before or after, ever attained such rulership. It rose to a point where enemies crawled at his heels for mercy. On these two occasions his magnanimity, always present in big things though absent in trifles, prevailed over ambition.

If he did have grand dreams of stupendous power, he kept them locked deep in the heart, and the world could only conjecture at the secret ambitions of this curious man and buzz with gossip over his desperate game, which for brilliancy of play and intensity of dramatic interest has never been equaled. Viewing the life of Old Hutch in the retrospect, his story seems to display with unusual vividness the universal subtle conflict of ambition and vanity with the wider and weaker claims of common good.

The Pit still howls as it howled in the stormy eighties. On its worn floors is the shuffle of a thousand feet. Around the quaint old building, a black granite pile that blocked the foot of LaSalle street, lofty temples of commerce have risen in recent years, sharpening the contrast of the old and the new. Like an etching each has stood out defiantly. As an act of safety, the tall tower, once the pride of the townfolk and the awe of the rustic, long ago was carved down to the belfry, from which a flock of doves was always startled by the booming of the gong. The line of hansom cabs, topped by proud pilots, that once fringed the street, has been replaced by a splash of garish taxis. Frock coats and silk tiles have given way to sack suits and rakish fedoras. Little remains in the street to mirror the romantic days of old, or to recall the chief actors of those riotous times. Even the old building itself is being replaced by a sky-towering edifice of stone.

The Pit still howls, but it is only a blurred echo out of a misty past. For the march of progress and a more discriminating society have shorn the Pit of its bad features and retained only the good. Today it is an essential part of commerce, a great artery through which the life-blood of trade is forever throbbing, steadily, normally.

Of all the strange actors that strutted its crowded stage in the olden days and scarred the Pit with their indiscretions, none rose to the glamorous heights of Old Hutch. His head-long, irrepressible genius tinted the fabric of speculation with a glow undimmed by time.

II

The Little Ship

A STRANGE and unrelenting fate seemed to pursue Benjamin P. Hutchinson during his boyhood and youth. As though marked by some unfathomable spell, he staggered under a burden of petty but disheartening reverses.

From childhood on he was feverishly engaged upon uncanny persistency. Swiftly he fell; slowly he rose acquired new and foreboding obstacles, and the misfortunes broke over his serious young head with an uncanny persistency. Swiftly he fell; slowly he rose to his feet; fell again, and slowly rose once more, laboriously setting to work restoring, stick by stick, his frail house of ambition.

In those hard New England days of a century ago, life was fraught with difficulties for the boy who mustered courage to strike out for himself. But this did not prevent young Ben from leaving the farm of his parents, near Danvers, Massachusetts, where he was born in 1829, and charting his own career while still in knee trousers.

Later in life he liked to recall those early days, but did so always with somewhat of a shudder. His distaste of farm life was immense. "To have made it my life's work, to have scratched away at the same fields from one year's end to another, would have been unutterably dreary. I should have felt like one of the woeful cows tethered to a stake, frozen in winter and tormented by flies in summer. Children of the soil in those days toiled bitterly from dawn to dark with back and hands and feet. Old age came as a mercy to lift the heavy burden of labor and of care. It meant leave to rest at last."

It was the winter that most embittered him against farm life. It began in late autumn. Powdery snow, whipped from the ground, drove across the brown lands and the clearings in blinding squalls and heaped itself behind whatever broke the force of the gale. To one side of the house it built a pointed tower, and between house and stable raised a drift six feet high, through which the shovel had to carve a path. But to windward the ground was bare, scoured by the driving blast. When the wind died down, myriad snowflakes sifted lazily from the skies, until the whole countryside became swallowed up in the great white blanket.

At night the fence rails were very black upon the white expanse palely lighted by the moon. Trunks of trees standing against the white background reminded the boy of skeletons of living creatures smitten with the cold and stricken by death. To him the glacial night was both awesome and affrighting.

During such days and nights the men scarcely left the house except to care for the beasts and came back on the run, their faces rasped with the cold and shining-wet with snow crystals melted by the heat of the house. Young Ben would pluck away the tiny globules that had knitted on his eye lashes, draw off his sheepskin coat, and settle himself by the stove, anxious to shut out all thought of the surrounding landscape.

To the boy, with an imagination that leaped and plunged and danced, the days were long and weary and the nights torturous. He was straining to get into the world, to become at least an incident in the big parade of life. On days when the wind had whipped a field clean, it was like sudden release from prison walls to go out into the cleared spaces and resume the interminable task of carrying and rolling rocks, big and small, to an ever-swelling pile behind the woodshed. The rocks in the fields seemed to grow like dandelions, multiplying in numbers with each season.

On other days there was the unspeakable woodpile to replenish. The stoves were like hungry beasts that gnawed eternally, and eternally remained starved. With stiff arms and low spirits he swung the ax hour after hour, having the eye and direction of an expert woodman. He detested the monotony far more than the effort. Always there was the same quick gleam of the descending blade as it caught the glare of the sun; always the same dull, deadly thud, followed by the whining of splinters as the dry wood separated. He felt that the monotony of no other task could be so depressing, so destroying to the mind. But he worked without complaint.

At last the longest winter known in the district was drawing to a close. The fields were warming up under the soft spring breeze, and the lingering patches of snow were vanishing even in the deep shade of the woods.

When the ice went out of the nearby stream, the lad walked up and down the creek, drawing a small boat tethered to a long string. He had fashioned the craft of firewood during long winter days, and called it "my little ship of hope."

As soon as the fields were ready for the plow, Benjamin took up the labor with an enthusiasm that filled his elders with pride. Under the misty blue skies he worked and sang and laughed, and in odd times whistled with the birds and raced with the dogs. He was happy because the plan he cherished, the plan to break from farm life, would soon be carried to conclusion. Long hours and hard tasks did not matter, and he kept up his part cheerfully until all the spring work was over. Then he went away, taking with him the "little ship of hope." To farm life he never returned.

In North Reading there lived a man named Edwin Foster, who was not only somewhat of a philosopher but also the shoe merchant of the town, and when dealing with commerce rather than philosophy he knew how to strike a neat bargain. It was to Mr. Foster that young Benjamin appealed for work.

"You look to be a likely boy," Mr. Foster admitted somewhat grudgingly. "You are tolerably tall and very large for your age. But in these days boys aren't what they used to be. It's just a gamble as to whether the temple is empty."

"Yes," young Ben agreed with a hidden twinkle, "that is the gamble each of us must take if we decide to go into business together."

There was nothing of the braggart about the lad, no

tinge of cocksureness. But he did have a calm, cold confidence, an unshakable belief in himself that was infectious.

The problem of engaging him was not one for quick decision, as Mr. Foster pointed out, and several meetings were necessary before the employer could form a conclusion.

"Well," he announced one day, "I've decided to take you in; I've decided to give you an opportunity in life that few boys of your age may ever hope for. You are to become my clerk. I want you to whirl in and make the store more attractive and more inviting. I want you to get about and meet all the young folks in town and meet their parents, too, and let them know the advantages of bartering at this institution. In a word, I shall expect you to increase the volume of sales. Now there will be odd times, moments of freedom which should not be permitted to escape. Wasting time is wasting life. During such moments I shall expect you to retire to the rear room and engage yourself upon the task of repairing shoes. You will find that work interesting as well as being a diversion from the other routine."

"Thank you, Mr. Foster; thank you for the offer; I will try to please you and prove my desire to get into trade. Now, you did not mention the matter of wages?"

"Oh, yes indeed," added the employer. "I mean to start you at twenty dollars———"

He paused, and the lad broke in:

"Twenty dollars a———"

"A year," said Mr. Foster. "Of course after a few month, if I find that you are not up to the work———"

"Of course I shall be," the boy interjected. But the enthusiasm had left his voice, and his throat seemed dry and heavy. He had hoped for something of greater promise, a quicker lane toward the vast land of dreams that seemed always to open up before his active vision.

But this was no time to quibble, and he entered upon his work with an earnestness and determination that provoked admiration. He was up and about bright and early; the most attractive merchandise was always on display; the cases and fixtures were dusted and polished until they shone, and all customers were given a hearty welcome by the lad, who invariably had some odd tale to tell or some delicious morsel of town gossip to pass along.

His instinct for trading developed with unusual rapidity. Those customers who found their tastes a bit beyond ready cash knew that young Benjamin was ever ready to bargain. If they were intrigued by a pair of boots which was past their immediate means, they might toss in with their cash a box of fruit, or some vegetables, or a sack or two of grain, or, perhaps, a calf or pig. No customer need go away empty handed. Ben would pay the difference in price out of his own thin purse and then dispose of the produce at will, and always at a profit. Mr. Foster was a bit puzzled by the shrewdness of the lad, but admired his ability for accumulating. Now and then it happened that in sizing up some prosperous out-of-town customer, Benjamin slipped the prices upward, and in doing so struck an extra dividend for his employer, who sharply rebuked the boy for such lapses, and at the same time patted him on the back and mentioned the value of sagacity.

For a long time all went well, and then there was discord. Young Ben discovered, through the dropping of a careless word, that another chap of less ability and less energy was receiving a salary of thirty dollars a year from Mr. Foster. He was enraged over this distinction. That night he expressed his sentiments in a notebook, in which he sometimes wrote verse, and which served as a sort of diary for his more unpleasant moods. He copied into the book long and dismal passages from Dante's *Divine Comedy*, with marginal comment and comparisons that would not have been complimentary to his employer.

By the following morning the mental storm had passed, however, and he was calm and determined. Likewise his plan of action was clear-cut and definite.

"I am resigning," he told his employer, simply, upon the latter's arrival at the store.

"Now, son, we can fix this thing up. You know that Jimmie gets about very early to make the mail ready for the mail coach to Boston. You know he reads writing hand more readily than you do. You know——"

"I know he's a friend of the family, and so you pay him more!"

"What do you plan on doing?" asked Mr. Foster when he saw the futility of trying to patch matters up.

"I'm going into business for myself."

"Well, son, you've given us many surprises but no real laughs before."

He soon learned that Benjamin was not joking, for in two days he had engaged a shed next door, paid three months' rent in advance, and had spread clear across the front a glaring sign inscribed: "Ben Hutchinson—Boots and Shoes." Thus did the greatest wheat plunger in history make his first plunge into commerce.

His little ship of hope rested on a shelf in the shop.

The townsfolk were elated over the lad's courage and registered their approval by turning patronage his way. And in the succeeding years he prospered far beyond expectation. In time he had several other young fellows working for him, running errands, cleaning the store, and doing the many odd jobs incident to the conduct of a growing business.

Every Saturday he would journey on foot to Lynn and dispose of shoes made during the week. He would likewise purchase stock with which to meet the needs of the following week. His instinct for trading made these trips profitable in many ways. He would always bring back with him a box of gimcracks that strongly appealed to the growing boys. Ben would trade these back and forth, back and forth, until by Monday morning he would have recovered from his youthful employees most of the money paid out to them during the week.

While he kept his expenses low, his love of chance led him into numerous pitfalls and on several occasions forced him to start almost at the bottom. But he was quick to wipe out losses, quick to adjust himself to new situations, and would go on as if no reverses had occurred.

By the time he reached twenty he had prospered handsomely and decided to leave the patched-up shed, with its brave inscription, and go to Lynn where he believed opportunity awaited him. Nor was his judgment wrong, for in that city he became a successful manufacturer of boots and shoes, created a large commission business in Boston, and within a comparatively short time had acquired a substantial fortune.

At about this time he met, wooed, and married the beautiful Sarah M. Ingalls, his one and only love, the woman who knew his every thought, dreamed his dreams, and, in his own words, made life a glowing inspiration. "The finest gift God could bestow upon man," was his tribute to this noble woman in the winter time of life.

For the next few years Benjamin Hutchinson "lived in the pink clouds of happiness." While his dislike of the unromantic shoe trade became almost an obsession, his domestic happiness was sublime.

Then of a sudden the blow fell. It swept all before it like a giant flail.

One day Mrs. Hutchinson returned home to find her husband white as death. He was shaken by a nerve storm and trembling in every limb. She spoke to him as he paced up and down the floor, face drawn and hands tightly clasped behind the back. He did not answer. Again she sought to question him and when he did not reply flung her arms about his neck.

He pointed to a message lying face up on a nearby stand. Mrs. Hutchinson snatched it up, read the contents, and then closing her eyes dropped into a chair. It was the year of 1857. And the message told of the financial revulsion which is still remembered for its disastrous results. It had made the Hutchinsons penniless. Worse still, it had caught Benjamin with his lines far extended, and failure of customers had heaped huge debts upon him. Only a few hours before he had been rich. Fate had struck its first hard blow.

Presently his pacing ceased, and he drew his wife to a couch, where they sat long in silence, staring vacantly at a blue patch of sky framed in the open doorway. The patch grew crimson, and at length a setting sun, full and red, crept into the frame.

The tall young man rose to his feet, pressed his wife closely in his arms, and whispered softly:

"Sarah, we're going to follow that sun. We're going west."

III

The Power of Wheat

THE cry for wheat has gone thundering down the dim corridors of time. .To obtain this life-giving food has been one of the major battles of man.

Back of Greece and Rome, and beyond Babylon, the romance of wheat may be sharply traced. It antedates Akkad and Sumer, and is older than Ur of the Chaldees. The struggle for this grain was hoary with years before the pyramids were built.

Instinct told the early man that the growing of wheat meant a more stable and plentiful food supply than could be found on the game trail. In the distant days of the Neanderthal man, wheat grains were raked into the soil, and the patchy crop crudely harvested. Ages later, as crops were expanded, there dawned a new and powerful idea. Nomads saw the wisdom of growing grain and of clustering in groups for mutual protection against natural and tribal enemies. Out of this ancient group idea the village was finally evolved, to be followed in time by the city and the state.

At first man pulled the wheat plants from the ground by hand. Then he learned to use a sharp flint or bone knife, a tool that gave way later to a blade of bronze. This straight instrument was replaced by the curved blade, an amazing innovation. The sickle of iron was fashioned by some unknown genius and grew into the scythe with a lengthened blade. Hundreds of years of merciless toil with the scythe and the cradle intervened before the birth of the horse-drawn reaper, the first of which was seen by men still living.

In the early days man carried his wheat to the threshing floor, where it was beaten out by the hoofs of half-tamed animals. Ages afterward came the flail. It served for centuries and remained in use in this country as late as the civil war.

In the course of time, fields began sprawling out over a wider and wider area. Yields became more bountiful. And across the skyline of history may be seen long caravans of camels laden with golden grain; the coracles of the Tigris or the Nile striving against mad currents to deliver the surplus wheat in exchange for fruits or fabrics of a distant tribe.

With this traffic came new knowledge of men and

things. Its expansion created a new geography. Wheat was money, and its ownership meant wealth with which to purchase jewels and precious silks and rare rugs and power and position. So the battle for wheat has been intense, feverish, and without end.

Wheat has been called the seed of civilization. It has scattered its bounties over the earth as nations rose and fell, as dynasties grew and faded, as savages became civil, and humanity more human. Wheat makes the world throb with industry; commerce is vivified with trade, transportation weighted; mills, elevators, and bakeries are made to vibrate with activity. From the misty time when women first powdered the grain between stones and mixed meal with water to cook over the glowing coals of a campfire, there marches the whole procession of humanity, from the near-man, guided by instinct, to the present civilization, guided and controlled by reason.

Benjamin Hutchinson knew wheat. And he loved wheat. "The very word always stimulated my mind," he said. "It churned my imagination. Wheat seems so powerful, so vital. There is a thrill in the feel of it, in taking up a handful and letting it sift through the fingers. And if you have ever walked alone through a field of ripening wheat, you may have some feeling of

its austere dignity, and its deep imposing solemnity.
Wheat is powerfully close to life."

A thirst for knowledge of wheat assailed Hutchinson
in his early youth, and his thirst was never quenched.
It haunted and tormented him throughout life. Before
he ever entered the Wheat Pit, his broad study had convinced him that the man who controls the supply of
essential food is in possession of almost supreme power.

There was, for instance, old Nomarch Henku, back
in the fifth Dynasty in Egypt, which historians place
at 2830 B. C., who had had inscribed on his tomb the
enviable though somewhat boastful line, "I was lord
and overseer of southern grain in this nome."

And then there was Joseph and his memorable
corner in grain. Joseph gathered and stored in years
of abundance one fifth of all the harvests. He knew
that the improvident Egyptians lived too lavishly and
laid by no stores against lean days. When famine put
its vicious hand upon the land, only one course was
open to the people. They had to go to Joseph. So also
did the people of nearby countries. They bought from
him until their funds were exhausted, but still they
suffered for want of nourishment. So they exchanged
cattle for grain, and when their cattle were gone they
bartered their lands and even themselves to ward off

starvation. As the price of life, Joseph reduced them to virtual slavery, after which he gave them food and put them back on the lands, on the condition of their paying a fifth as tribute to him, by virtue of his prerogative. Then he enjoined them to the same diligence as if they were to derive the emolument resulting from the whole. They resumed work with such assiduity that Joseph, by his well-timed act, established his own authority in Egypt, and increased the standing revenue of all its succeeding monarchs.

In the writings of Mencius, who was born in 372 B. C., may be found something of the power that comes to the owner of wheat. He complains to King Hui of Laing that when grain is so abundant that the dogs and swine eat the food of man, proper collections for storage are not made. "And when people are dying from famine on the roads, you do not issue the stores of your granaries for them. When they thus die and you say, 'It is not owing to me; it is owing to the year,' in what does this differ from stabbing and killing a man, and then saying, 'It was not I; it was the weapon'?"

A knowledge of the intricacies of wheat commerce was deemed one of the qualities of a statesman in Athens, where the speculative practice of those long-headed men able to forecast the future often drew factions to the brink of civil war. Lysias made his famous oration against the speculators of Athens, the great wheat mart of the eastern Mediterranean, in 387 B. C., throwing light upon the futile attempts of the government to prevent corners or to control prices. "For when you happen to be most in want of grain, the speculators have it and are unwilling to sell. You may be well satisfied to buy from them at any price whatever and take your leave of them, so that sometimes when there is peace we are reduced to a state of siege by them."

And so it goes throughout history. Rome made a colossal experiment in fixing prices that utterly failed; Great Britain had bread price laws for over a century, repealing them for their futility; Antwerp was overthrown in 1558, due largely, say historians, to setting prices; revolutionary France sought to drive off the speculator by fixing prices, and the protagonists of the movement perished on the guillotine.

Hutchinson knew the stories in detail and told them with fervor.

When he decided to enter the Wheat Pit and begin his long uphill drive toward mastery he was an exceptional student of wheat history, ancient and modern.

Minute details of production, distribution, and world needs were filed away in his big analytical brain. He knew that traffic in this grain covered the earth by every means of transportation, and that yet there was want and suffering for lack of wheat. He knew that of the total land area, that producing wheat was relatively small, although it is the most adaptable of grains, and may be made to grow from the tropics to the Arctic circle.

After the revulsion of 1857 that swept away his fortune and plunged him deep into debt, Hutchinson came from Massachusetts to Chicago, stopping for a time in Milwaukee, which he ironically termed "a city with neither inspiring energy nor imagination."

Chicago was then an ugly little town, just beginning to dig itself out of the mud. It had recently built its first city waterworks to replace the primitive system that sent sand, weeds, minnows, and pollywogs through the faucets to the dinner table. The Illinois Central railway project and other big new enterprises were going bravely forward. Emigrants were pouring into the railroad lands, just as wheat, corn, and live stock were pouring in from southern Illinois and bulging the sides of groaning Chicago. Solid city streets were replacing the mudholes in which drays, wagons, and stage-coaches might often be seen wallowed deep and abandoned, bearing curious signs by local wits, such as "Man lost here," and "Shortest route to China." In four years the town had spent twenty millions in building operations, and a second boom was on, a boom that shot land values skyward and made the most icy-hearted real estate gentlemen blush at the thought of their ill-earned profits.

Remote settlements on the lakes and on the Mississippi were awaiting only the shriek of the locomotive to stir them to life and to draw them into the Chicago trade. Minnesota had just been admitted to the Union, and, like other states in the district, paid increasing tribute to Chicago by sending grain, cattle, and lumber, and buying in return manufactures and imports. Fewer and fewer wagon caravans came to town, but wheat arrived by the carload, and elevators were rapidly displacing warehouses. Drovers were no longer seen in numbers, but every railroad had its stockyards for the unloading and sale of cattle and hogs.

Chicago was being transformed from a retail to a wholesale town, the trade center between the factories of the East and the farms of the Northwest.

"I tell you, Sarah, it is the city of the future," Hutchinson declared after spending a few days looking into the varied activities. He related fabulous tales of what was happening and outlined the grand dreams of the future. He told of the many improvements underway, including the project of raising all houses and business blocks in certain districts to bring them more safely above the lake level.

There was, for instance, the Tremont House, where Lincoln sometimes held forth, a four story structure of brick and stone, and one of the skyscrapers of Chicago in the fifties. As the intersecting streets began to rise by reason of the grading project, this hostelry had to build steps down to its somewhat magnificent dining room. Stories in the East told how the building was sinking in a bottomless morass, to the great distress of the owners.

Then one day a young man guest from New York appeared and asked for the job of raising the building.

"What makes you think you could do it?" the doubtful proprietors questioned.

"Well, I've raised buildings along the line of the Erie canal, and I can raise anything if I can get enough jackscrews under it. About five thousand of them would do for this job."

"You'd simply wreck the building!"

"I'll contract to pay for every pane of glass broken."

"Anyhow, the guests would be scared to death and leave."

"They won't know it! They won't miss a meal or a wink of sleep."

"All right, go ahead. What's your name, young man?"

"George M. Pullman."

Chicago was beginning to make names.

George M. Pullman of Pullman car fame covered the basement with heavy timbers upon which he set the five thousand jackscrews. At these he placed twelve hundred and fifty men, or one to each four screws. At a given signal the building began to rise, inch by inch, until the desired height was attained. Reports of the remarkable feat went clattering over the wires to eastern newspapers and started that section buzzing with tales of how the little giant of the West was pulling itself out of the mud by its own bootstraps.

Hutchinson told and retold the story. It was typical of the times. Everyone was doing new and strange things. There was intense, feverish activity. The city was alive, alert, straining to break its bonds and conquer new fields.

Already there were heard half-hearted boasts that Chicago was the natural grain market, and was destined to control wheat traffic of the entire world. Hutchinson was one of the few who steadfastly believed that this would come to pass.

For several weeks he watched the river of golden grain flow into the city. He studied the restless throngs who were buying and selling. Then he purchased a membership in the Wheat Pit, not for ten thousand dollars, but for a ten dollar bill.

He was pipping at the shell of a greater destiny.

IV

Mysterious Stranger

HE was lean, amazingly tall, and very striking in appearance. Many people thought him remarkably good looking, while others considered him almost ugly. But there was no one who ignored him, no one who forgot to see him when he was present. He was powerfully built, and advanced straight at you, head slightly forward, eyes cold and motionless.

While still in robust youth he became known as Old Hutch, perhaps by reason of his solemn mien, his long, unsmiling silences, and his unfailing self-possession. His face was strong, clean-shaven, with powerful features. The nose was hooked like the beak of an eagle, and arbitrary, the chin prominent and determined, and the mouth well-shaped, with lines suggesting a suppressed sense of humor. Under a sweep of darkish brows, the narrow eyes shone out steady and

Old Hutch

fearless. There were times when they softened and seemed full of delicate and almost lazy irony.

About the great bony man there was the air of an aristocrat, an adventurer who had seen many lands and who had known men and life. His voice was a bit harsh and grating, particularly in rare moments of passion, but it was a voice that reflected strength of character and seemed somehow to belong to the huge frame. Usually it was grave and deep and convincing. His words were sparse in those early days, for he knew the value of keeping his own counsel.

Not even for a moment did Old Hutch give the impression that he was sensitive, that is, in the sense of shrinking ever so slightly from an opinion that might be adverse or even hostile to him. Never did he seem to be on the defensive in those early years of his career. In his calm, unruffled way he strolled about the trading floor, observing every move and making mental note of every action. And remaining as silent as a sphinx.

To many traders he was somewhat of an enigma; his quick grasp of a situation and his evident background of knowledge—as to cause and effect—were puzzling and confusing, and at first they referred to him as the mysterious stranger, the new-comer who seemed to have inside information on every move of the market.

At the time Old Hutch launched his career in the Wheat Pit, excitement permeated all lines of business and industry. The air was filled with uncertainty. For several years division between the north and the south on the slavery question had been bitter. It seemed that each new event fanned the flames of dissension—the discovery of gold in California and the adoption by that state of a free-soil constitution; the sensational appearance of Mrs. Stowe's "Uncle Tom's Cabin"; the bloody fight between pro-slavery and free-soil men in Kansas; and John Brown's grotesque raid at Harper's Ferry.

But this excitement was tame compared with that which burst forth at the opening of hostilities.

Food supplies were in demand. Speculation became rampant. Fortunes were made and lost in a tornado of buying and selling. The gold market whipped about violently, its desperate fluctuations rushing wheat prices up and down regardless of fundamental conditions.

Suddenly Old Hutch found his vast knowledge of wheat somewhat neutralized. Supply and demand and future prospects meant little under the disgraceful manipulation of gold prices. But Old Hutch was adaptable. Almost over night he changed his whole mode of campaign. He had the genius of a lightning-fast speculator who could change with the tide, and he rapidly brought that faculty into play, discarding his intensive study of world wheat conditions in favor of a study of gold.

"It was my immediate purpose," he said many years later, "to create a fortune, pay off my haunting debts in Massachusetts, and have a fund adequate for large speculative drives."

This he proceeded to do. He observed the course of gold prices far more closely than the factors that normally control the price of wheat, and in all his trades he was guided accordingly.

His finances were so small that he was compelled to build gradually and with utmost care. He understood fully and acted upon the first half of Ricardo's judicious maxim, "Cut short your losses." Whenever he scented danger he ran; and thus, dollar by dollar, his fund grew to a point where the volume of trades took on a tone of dignity.

During the first two years of operation his painstaking study of gold prices enabled him to accurately anticipate the trend of the wheat market. He bought small amounts when wheat prices started upward, and sold quickly when signs pointed to a downward plunge, which happened with considerable frequency by reason of the manipulation of gold.

His first substantial profit came in 1863, when he anticipated the revenue tax on liquors. So confident was he in his judgment that he assumed a greater risk than he had hitherto dared to take. And the profits chalked up were a tribute to his ability to "think ahead of the crowd."

This single speculative turn seemed to form the basis for greater activity. That is, Old Hutch now felt that he was beyond the danger line, financially, and with a series of swift, sure strokes he began his minor drives upon the market.

Magical changes had been wrought by the war. They were economic as well as social. One of them reached out into the grain markets. There was created, during the conflict, the nucleus of the present Wheat Pit. The government had wanted to erase all doubt as to definite supplies at certain future dates. At the same time it desired to shift the risk to a single responsible individual instead of scattering large contracts among a number of Chicago men.

One man did assume the enormous risk of the government contract, but he immediately interested a number of other men and thus succeeded in spreading the responsibility among many. These other men agreed to deliver to him at certain future dates specific amounts of grain at stipulated prices. The aggregate volume equaled the government contract.

Such were the first contracts in grain futures—the life-blood of the Wheat Pit. And so successfully did the plan serve society that it became a natural economic part of American commerce.

But the system early lent itself to flagrant speculative flights, and during the period of greatest intensity the dark shadow of Old Hutch may be seen constantly gliding back and forth upon the stage, a symbol of speculative shrewdness and daring.

It was during the momentous year of 1864 that the power of Old Hutch began to be felt. In the course of two months wheat advanced twenty-four cents. He had purchased as many "contracts" for future delivery as his funds would safely permit. On the tide of rising prices he unloaded his holdings, and the rank and file of traders, swept by the waves of tempestuous emotion, were eagerly buying when Old Hutch was ready to sell.

Not only did he sell his wheat near the top prices,

but he followed this by selling "short," anticipating a drastic fall in prices which would duplicate the handsome profits accumulated on the rise. In this belief he was alone, his judgment pitted against that of the crowd.

"What reason have you to believe prices will drop?" he was asked over and over again. But he remained silent.

For the next few months his apparent blunder was the gossip of the Pit, and those who had struck up a sort of distant friendship bolstered their courage and suggested to Old Hutch that the market would undoubtedly continue to go against him and perhaps wipe out all of his early gains.

"I have neither asked nor offered advice," was his smiling reply. And facing about, he strolled leisurely away.

One of the more persistent traders followed and asked:

"But what sound basis can you have for expecting a break?"

Old Hutch slackened his pace, turned his head slightly, and over one shoulder snapped out the words:

"Gold! War!"

Then he was off, while the little group of puzzled traders shook their heads doubtfully.

It was not long until the course of the gold market had its depressing effect on wheat. Prices began to weaken. Then they broke sharply. In the scramble that ensued Old Hutch was nowhere to be seen. His lines had been carefully laid, and he was free to assume an attitude of indifference. Events were bearing out the first part of his prediction.

Strength crept back into the market a few days later, but was of short duration. A more extreme influence was close at hand.

The Pit was not unaccustomed to war news of paramount importance. It had been tossed into turmoil and shaken like a quake on several occasions. But it was hardly prepared for the electrifying announcement of the victories at Gettysburg and Vicksburg. Such news was followed by sensational gyrations in gold prices and a simultaneous smash in the wheat market. By the time August arrived, war-time wheat was selling for eighty cents a bushel.

And it was reported that Old Hutch had bought in his "short" wheat around that figure. His prediction that gold and war would knock the bottom out of the wheat market during that crop season had been confirmed.

When the eventful year of 1864 drew to a close, with the gold dollar worth two dollars and twenty-six cents, Benjamin P. Hutchinson was enjoying high prosperity. And when he shook hands with and congratulated General Sherman and General U. S. Grant on the occasions of their respective visits to the exchange the following June, he was a man of considerable means.

His very first act after accumulating a fortune was to pay off all debts in Massachusetts, adding a substantial rate of interest for the period of duration. No one had ever questioned that he would do just that sort of thing, for he was reputed extraordinarily honest, a man of his word, and his word was never questioned.

This course of clearing up old debts was greatly to his credit, and gave him an enviable standing. In a period of five years he had acquired enough money to wipe out the innumerable eastern obligations and retain a fortune of fair proportion. Old timers around the trading ring commented dryly that "the mysterious stranger had been getting on."

Let it not be thought that Old Hutch prospered

simply by reason of the war. He would have done much better in peace times, as later events proved. The war only added new hazards and made more difficult the task of anticipating the course of prices. Risk of speculation was far greater than in normal times. When the war came to a close, Chicago was firmly entrenched in the position she had won during the conflict, as the greatest primary market in the world for the two indispensable foods—bread and meat.

"It is only the beginning," Hutch used to say in those post-war times. "It is just the dawn of a new era. As surely as the sun rises, Chicago will some day be the bread and meat center of the entire world."

Up to the time Hutch acquired a safe fortune with which to carry on his speculative exploits, he had shown no particular pride of opinion. He would switch from one side of the market to the other in a twinkling, being both bull and bear while the clock ticked off a single minute. No man ever had a keener perception of what the trading crowd was doing; nor was any one ever more fully informed of the smoldering plans of the big operators. At first the more powerful speculators sought to chastise him, and on several occasions his doom was near at hand, but somehow, some way, he always contrived to wriggle out of their net.

He had built his initial fortune not by connivance with others, but by working alone, silently, dismally, taking little or no part in the general camaraderie that pervades the trading floor. He was a prime scalper, and like a flash would get in and out of the market. Only two or three times up to 1866 did he take a solid position and patiently await the turn of events, and in these instances his judgment was justified.

An opportunity arose in 1866 which was reported to have augmented the growing fortune of Old Hutch. For weeks he watched the price of wheat climb steadily until it reached the pinnacle of a dollar ninety on July ninth. Old Hutch had refrained from buying wheat, for he knew that a small group had been engineering a corner and that they were not sufficiently strong to withstand any sudden bolt that might strike the market. Hutch knew that the time was rapidly approaching when something would happen to burst the bubble, and accordingly he sold "short" large quantities of wheat with the expectation of buying back these "contracts" at a lower figure.

A few minutes before the day's trading began one bright day in that same month, Old Hutch strolled quietly into the exchange hall. There was an atmosphere of suppressed excitement. Every one was inquiring of his neighbor whether news of importance had developed. Messenger boys raced in and out with colored order slips; call bells were jangling, and brokers and clerks hurrying to their accustomed places.

Suddenly the gong boomed out, signaling the start of the day's business. There was a brief spasm of excited buying and selling, and then the market went stale. But the air seemed charged with expectancy, a feeling that often reflects itself upon the speculative markets prior to some extraordinary event.

There was not long to wait, for almost at the same fraction of a second a dozen wild-eyed men, followed by spindle-legged messengers, came rushing toward the ring of traders in the Pit.

News of the great Prussian victories over Austria was out.

This news meant a speedy ending of the war. It meant a smaller demand for wheat. It likewise meant trouble for those who were attempting to maintain a corner.

But of immediate interest to Old Hutch, it meant the price of wheat was tumbling to a point where he might cover his short sales at handsome profits and cut another notch in the stock of his speculative gun. This he did.

Old Hutch was now ready for real business, business on a broad scale. Up to this time he had been handicapped by lack of capital. His efforts were necessarily confined to small deals. As a matter of safety he had permitted opportunities to pass him by. He had not felt ready.

But now a strange song seemed to drum in his ears, provocative and tremendous. He felt its glamorous influence night and day. He yearned to throw himself into the adventure of which he had dreamed, to match his skill and wisdom with the combined power of the crowd.

At length a chance offered itself. The wheat crop in 1866 was not as large as had been expected. Its quality was excellent, and this sharpened the demand. Merchants sold heavily and shipped large quantities into Ohio, Indiana, and Pennsylvania, where it was said the crop was gradually dying out.

By reason of these heavy shipments the contract wheat in the regular warehouses at Chicago during the next spring gradually dwindled to one million bushels.

Old Hutch was convinced the time was propitious to try what had been deemed the impossible. He began deftly laying his lines, working alone, and keeping his scheme heavily veiled by an outward show of minor activities.

Slowly, quietly, he bought up the one million bushels in the warehouses. Then he proceeded to purchase all the options that others desired to sell. His operation was extended over a considerable period, for any attempt at rapid execution would have revealed and destroyed the scheme.

For weeks the unsuspecting bears continued to pour wheat into the hands of Old Hutch, confident that the prevailing high prices could not continue and that there would be plenty of wheat with which to cover their short contracts when delivery day arrived.

But as that day of reckoning approached there was little wheat to be had. Prices began rising in a fashion that erased all doubt as to what was under way. A flurry of excitement quickly grew into a panic as the bears tried to fight their way out of the trap. As a dramatic climax wheat shot up to two dollars and eighty five cents, one of the highest figures in history.

Within the hour Old Hutch acquired the respect shown a visiting archbishop and became "Mr. Hutchinson" to the crowd. He sent word that they would be permitted to see him at a certain time for the purpose of settling their contracts. They appeared at the appointed hour, meek and respectful. When a settlement had been made the price of wheat plunged downward fifty cents in a single hour and sixty-five cents in a day.

The trick had been turned, and Old Hutch was the acknowledged king of the Pit. He had driven wheat up seventy-five cents in thirty days, had forced the over-confident bears to settle at his own price, and had, incidentally, boosted his fortune into the seven-figure class.

It was the first important corner in the history of the Wheat Pit.

The artistry with which Old Hutch had operated made the trick look easy. So the next year John B. Lyon ran a corner with moderate success. For a period of four years the same operator tried it again. But he lacked the finesse. Moreover the West had been growing. There was more wheat. Lyon did not know how to control it. His attempted corners went to smash ruinously.

"Corners are a thing of the past."

Such was the nation's verdict after the Lyon failure.

Old Hutch smiled. And went on dreaming his dream.

V

The Taint

BURSTING upon the public like a rocket, news of the raid by Old Hutch created a storm of bitter protest. He was roundly denounced as an intolerable tyrant, a living firebrand spreading chaos among those charged with the holy duty of distributing the nation's food supply.

Fuel was added to the flame by those unhappy speculators who had been banged about, battered, and disfigured financially in the vise with which Old Hutch had squeezed them.

For a few months the bitterness continued at fever heat, during which time Old Hutch, patiently, perhaps joyously, trod the martyr's path amid the cackling ribaldry of an angry public. Then the storm blew over, as such storms do, and he became a sort of national hero. The press praised his genius and daring, reserving the right to administer an occasional public spanking for his apparent "lack of ethics."

"Ethics!" grumbled Old Hutch, his patience at last sorely tried. "The word has a curious rattle. Its meaning is hardly known in business today. Yet no one has accused me of violating any laws; nor have I been charged with failing to observe the hard and fast rules of the game. What I have done may likewise be tried by anyone who wishes to risk his fortune. The field is open to all.

"I have issued no spurious stock certificates, stolen no railroads, joined in no gold conspiracy. For a study of such type of 'ethics' I would respectfully invite your attention to the gentlemen of Wall Street."

Old Hutch was right. In those days Wall Street reeked with speculative outrages. Raw as grain speculation was; blatant as it was, tawdry as it was, it yet reflected a certain wholesomeness when compared with the crimson parade of Wall Street. To get a true picture of the period, which was crowded with dramatic episodes, it is only necessary to turn to the history of 1869.

The harvest of the war seemed to be wild extravagance, loose morals, rotten business, and filthy politics. Huge deals were planned; immense speculations carried on. Panics convulsed Wall Street, and the world

Daniel Drew
At the helm of the ship of stock speculation in the late sixties
stood the picturesque figure of Uncle Dan'l Drew.

stared in amazement at the enormous fortunes won and lost. Crooked bookkeeping, stock watering, blind pooling, and inside unloading were as continuous as they were unrestrained. Ring leaders, instead of hearing the clank of prison gates for their misdeeds, went merrily ahead with their unsavory exploits.

With the war a wretched memory, and reconstruction under way, the West had begun booming; factories of New England were whirling with life; the South was visualizing a new dawn, and the national financial center throbbed with activity. Politics were gorging out of the hand of Wall Street, and Wall Street was inviting every man to become a speculative glutton. At the helm of the ship of stock speculation stood the picturesque figures of Drew, Gould, Fisk, and Vanderbilt.

As Old Hutch dryly commented, "Try to find the ethics."

By the spring of that year thin iron rails had crawled across the continent, and the first railroad train moved from the Atlantic to the Pacific, providing new excuse for making rail stocks the football of speculation.

And before the year ended, the hysteria had been climaxed by Black Friday, a notorious stain on the pages of financial history.

The eyes of the whole country suddenly blinked at Wall Street spectacles. Horrified at the sight, the conservative Atlantic Monthly gave more space that year to adventures in Wall Street than it gave to such shining stars as Whittier, Lowell, Howells, Holmes, and Henry James.

"The brightest class are men of strong mind and weak morals, supreme egotists," wrote Henri Junius Browne in revealing some of the colorful deeds for that publication. "They glitter constantly and in these piping times of peace, seek commercial triumphs and financial crowns, and their natural field is Wall Street.

"The magnitude of Wall Street's operations and the reckless spirit of its operators attract at first and fascinate at last. They crave the excitement of corners, the bull and bear lockings-up, involving millions. It is to them a daily intoxication. To wealth they grow indifferent. At first the end, it soon becomes the means. Love of power and sensation drives them on when mere avarice has long been sated.

"Many of the present leaders of Wall Street have been in very different callings. They have been cattle drivers, ferrymen, chair-makers, peddlers, and horse jockeys. They have extraordinary ability of a certain kind, understand human nature, and believe in the commercial advantage of unscrupulousness. The financial magnate is now more adventurous than ever before. Each month seems to render him more reckless, more dishonest actually. Jacob Little used to make country people stare by the stupendousness of his operations and suddenness of his combinations, but he never forfeited his reputation for financial integrity, he never dreamed of doing what is now done in Wall Street daily without compunction and without criticism.

"Speculation in the banking quarter to-day means making money by any means that will not lead to the penitentiary. Success preserves from the necessity of offending in the common way; terms are dictated to fortune.

"Yet how few of Wall Street's financial adventurers have any permanent success! Those who were powers and radiating influences ten years ago have sunk out of sight and are forgotten. Hardly a great name on the Stock Exchange today was heard of twenty years ago. Monetary kings rise and fall with the rapidity of South America's revolutionary heroes; and once down, the most sensitive echo does not murmur that they have ever been. They are used as pawns by the greater players who let them move about for a while, then exchange them as the game grows interesting, or ruthlessly sweep them from the board.

"They learn nothing in Wall Street by experience. Each fancies himself wiser than his predecessors, trusts his own thoughts and destiny more, and then is ruined in exactly the same way. They seem to become victims of great surprises; they lie down honest in intention; they awake revolutionized out of a windy dream. Their hopefulness is always beyond their executive capacity, and intense desires strangle their conscientiousness. However much they may be in the dark to-day, they fondly dream they will be in the full tide of radiance to-morrow. They are not wholly dishonest; they are cut by a broad pattern. And this type does not fret or whine if he throws double deuces instead of double sixes."

For the span of two decades poor old Erie Railroad provided the chief sensations and outrages of Wall Street. There were flurries, panics, receiverships, and reorganizations. The history of Erie from the time Daniel Drew entered the directory in 1852 until driven from the presidency by main force in 1872 is replete with surprises. Drew was in control of the road until 1868. For years Commodore Vanderbilt, who had obtained control of the Harlem, the Hudson, and the New York Central, fought desperately with Drew in the legislature, the courts, and the stock market in an effort to wrest away mastery of the Erie. Drew finally lost, but Vanderbilt did not gain control, for the road passed into the hands of Gould, who for four years made it the plaything of his operations.

At the time Old Hutch became a national hero, or a national menace, depending upon the point of view, Jay Gould, Bill Tweed and Jim Fisk were concluding their Erie bout with August Belmont and Daniel Drew, pocketing fortunes by manipulations that kept courts and legislatures buzzing with activity.

The day arrived when Mr. Belmont thought he could snatch control away from Gould, depending for his strength upon foreign holders. His confidence was so great that he felt constrained to announce details of reforms he intended introducing. One of them was a readjustment of the company's capital stock.

Those oily gentlemen on the other side of the war, and yet in possession, seized upon the hint as an opportunity to clean up. They contended that if August Belmont really had a majority, as claimed, there was indeed an urgent reason for readjusting the capital, and expanding the voting supply.

But why, argued Gould and Fisk, take Belmont's word offhand? There were too many tiresome formalities involved in the increasing of capital stock. A much quicker way would be to buckle in on the theory that Belmont was doing a bit of bragging.

So they hurried to a judge of the supreme court who was amazed at their tale of Belmont's audacity; he agreed that they were the proper guardians of Erie credit. He went even further and empowered these fearless protectors of the railroad to adopt a course that would insure safety. The court permitted them as trustees to make a little investment. They were authorized to go into the market and purchase some Erie shares—two hundred thousand of them—not for themselves; dear me, no; but for the maintenance of the independence of poor old Erie from the plot of stock jobbers. And they turned the trick, causing Erie stock, then in the forties, to somersault into the sixties! Those worthy chatelains of Erie netted a million and a quarter dollars. And in addition they kept the management.

During these years of Erie's ups and downs, securities were issued by the bushel, legislatures were bribed, law became a means for plunder, and the courts ran riot through the legal webs spun by opposing factions. Injunctions and counter-injunctions could be bought like butter and eggs. In a spontaneous uprising of the people, two corrupt judges were driven from the bench.

Drew's trick of issuing new stock and flooding the market with it, and then by divers means preventing its transfer on the books, so as to retain control of the road, was copied by Gould, who was a still greater master of speculation. To prevent repetition of this scandal the stock exchange finally adopted a rule requiring shares of companies to be registered. At first Gould refused to comply, Fisk and Drew joining him in calling it a fine outrage for a pack of stock brokers to be parading such supervisory airs. The idea that any one should presume to interfere with the sacred rights of the insiders to trim the other fellow!

The sharp answer of the Stock Exchange was to strike Erie from the list. Such peremptory action brought these angry gentlemen to time.

"Freebooters are not extinct," wrote Charles Francis Adams of the Erie deals. "Gambling is a business now, where formerly it was a disreputable excitement." The issuance of convenient new stock he called "The most extraordinary feat of financial legerdemain which history has yet recorded."

Mr. Gould was finally driven from the Erie presidency under a revolt inspired chiefly by English stockholders. He was sued for nearly ten million claimed to have been converted to his own use from road assets.

After being under arrest for a short time he made his famous "restitution," turning over some real estate and securities valued nominally at six million dollars. But they were really worth only two hundred thousand dollars, as shown later in sworn testimony before the Hepburn railroad committee.

Here is another incident typical of the business ethics of the dying sixties. Cornelius Vanderbilt was educating the investor and the speculator in the fine points of his incubating New York Central. For the benefit of the public he sorrowed enormously over the heartless ways of opposing politicians. But he could not awaken Wall Street sympathy. Instead of helping devise relief for the road against the scolding law makers, those ridiculous folks in the Street banged away at Central every time it dared raise its head. They argued that a stock had no right to sell above one thirty when its own official spokesman bewailed the uncertainty of dividends.

It was indeed a dull day when Central fell only a fraction under the wallops of the short interests, who were predicting that Vanderbilt and his interests would soon be dropped unceremoniously upon the scrap heap.

Then one Saturday the stock shot up four points.

But the shorts were not frightened or intimidated by what they called Vanderbilt's eleventh hour flare of fight. They went on selling short.

There was somewhat of a shock, however, when an official Central bulletin right after the close of the exchange announced the fixing of a cash dividend rate of four per cent. This, said the shorts, was indeed super-audacity on the part of Vanderbilt in prolonging his misery. So more short sales were made wherever brokers met over the week-end.

When the stock exchange opened the next Monday morning, Commodore Vanderbilt favored the public with a postscript to his four per cent cash dividend. The subsequent groans echoed for years through the Street. It was a simple little postscript, merely announcing: "Also declared a scrip dividend of eighty per cent." Central shot up thirty points; then followed another forty points before the Commodore was through chastising the Street and pocketing a fortune.

By way of observing the ethics of the times, Old Hutch liked to call attention to another little railroad war of 1869 that weighed heavily upon the public purse. It was feudalism in the last degree and revolved about the Albany & Susquehanna Railway, a side line stretching across New York from Binghamton to Albany. Joseph Ramsey was the founder of the project. The starting point hooked to Erie's terminals at Binghamton.

Only after he had sold a good part of his stock did Ramsey learn that Erie was the buyer and intended to vote him out at the annual election. To some friendly judges he rushed for a pocketful of injunctions and mandamuses and for the use, when need be, of state police batallions. Jay Gould also knew a great many judges, and they had no hesitancy in arming him with new and rustling legal documents.

President Ramsey was none of your wishy-washy rail executives. He knew how to fight fire with fire. So he proceeded to steal the company's books from himself and hide them in a graveyard out in Ohio.

Mr. Gould was just as full of surprises. He deliberately picked a fresh set of books out of the air and certified himself as the rightful successor, with all the legal seals and judicial flourishes that could be collected by a gluttonous collector.

Both sides gained adherents until the noisy warfare exploded in the great open spaces. The climax was to be a try-out of corporation law. Ramsey commandeered a company locomotive, puffing and grinding and fully manned, and raced to Albany. Mr. Gould, not to be outdone, ordered a bigger engine, coaled and fired, and shouted above the tumult: "Not a stop till Binghamton!"

This somewhat unethical game of stealing the Albany & Susquehanna from each other had a sort of O'Henry ending. An outside judge passed the railroad over to an outsider in the battle, the Delaware and Hudson. Mr. Gould turned his restless mind to other matters, while Mr. Ramsey seemed satisfied with meagre fame. A little station on the Erie railway bears his name.

Black Friday, the super-climax of the 1869 debacle, was one of the most extraordinary days in Wall Street history. It was the culmination of the notorious gold conspiracy. Jay Gould was the shining star in those speculative skies, surrounded by a number of dimmer satellites.

Black Friday was the bursting of an intrigue, discovered and doomed before the conspiracy had been given its final touches. The scheme was conceived in the mind of Gould. Boisterous, blundering Jim Fisk was the cause of the discovery. Gould had prepared a logical argument in defense of the undertaking. At that time American farm commodities were paid for abroad in gold. A bushel of wheat at two dollars gold in England, which was setting world prices, meant more and more United States currency, as gold might yield a premium. At parity the farmer received two dollars. At fifty per cent premium his grain stood him at three dollars. At a hundred per cent premium it brought four dollars American money. The scheme smacked of high patriotism.

But blatant Jim Fisk spurned such pretense. He did not crave the role of benefactor to the down-trodden son of the soil.

"Hell!" was his blunt but candid comment. "There ain't any gold. We've cornered it all. Come on, boys; whoop 'er up!"

Meantime Gould had continued his argument that an advance in the premium of gold would stimulate exports of wheat and benefit the farmer, believing, too, that the treasury would suspend its sales of gold. And this for a time was the treasury policy.

Gould's bull pool rushed up the premium twelve points. Fisk, aflame with the heat of speculation, had pushed a crazy henchman into the Gold Room to bid for any amount at any price. That one broker accumulated contracts to the sum of twenty three million dollars, the shouts of Fisk, like the cracking of a whip, driving him from fever to fever.

Other members of the pool liquidated, leaving Gould and Fisk to carry on the deal.

The order that shattered the corner came like a bolt. It took the form of a telegram which Secretary Boutwell sent on instruction from President U. S. Grant. It said simply:

"Sell four millions gold and buy four millions bonds."

Like an avalanche the news swept into the Gold Room with terrible violence. New terror was unleashed. Operators old at the game lost their heads and dashed hatless and crazed through the streets, eyes bloodshot and brains afire; the crowd in New Street became a mob. The price of gold plunged downward thirty points. Transactions, amounting to over four hundred million dollars, could not be cleared by the Gold Exchange Bank, and clearances were suspended for a month, and gold dealings for a week.

In this giant of fiascos, with its savage and sensationally criminal methods and its ghastly consequences, Gould used fifty brokers; the contracts of one, which totaled thirty seven million dollars, being repudiated.

"The malign influence which Catiline wielded over the reckless and abandoned youth of Rome," said James A. Garfield, as head of a congressional committee, "finds a fitting parallel in the power which Fisk held in Wall Street, when, followed by the thugs of Erie and the debauchees of the opera, he swept into the Gold Room and defied both the Street and the United States Treasury."

Black Friday was made the subject of the poem by E. C. Stedman, banker-poet, beginning:

> "Zounds! How the price went flashing through
> Wall Street, William, Broad Street, New!
> All the specie in all the land
> Held in a ring by a giant hand—
> For millions now it was ready to pay
> And throttle the Street on Hangman's day."

Pleasant days, those. And as Old Hutch pointed out, "extremely ethical."

It was a gay, hard era, that post-war period. The brilliant, cruel pageant of Wall Street was at the pinnacle of its glory, and the hearts of men were burning with greed. Speculation was a machine-rattling, God-mocking game. Its prolongment would have meant national disaster.

Voices were raised against the whole disgraceful system. Those uttering the protests and demanding reforms were like criers in the wilderness.

VI

A Flaming City

THROUGH his trades in wheat Old Hutch himself may have profited indirectly by the gold conspiracy. But there is nothing in the records to confirm this belief. And certainly there is no evidence hinting that he participated directly in the gold conspiracy, or in any other unclean or illegal speculative trickery. On the contrary he was a sworn, eternal enemy of trumped-up schemes for shady group action. He scorned them, as if convinced that that were the only decent thing to do. His dislike of cliques and pools was inborn and immense. He detested them as he detested certain formalities and conventions; just as he hated that unscrupulous humbug, the professional politician. He never stated his reasons or made excuses for his likes or dislikes. Nor did any one seem to feel he should do so. Old Hutch and his many eccentricities, which multiplied in later life, were accepted without question.

Every one knew that at heart he was honest, courageous, and ready to battle for right, regardless of where the blows might fall. This may seem paradoxical in light of his cruel and vicious attacks upon markets and the unrelenting stranglehold with which he seized those speculators who dared block his path. But the life of Old Hutch was in itself somewhat of a paradox.

It rarely happens that a genius of extraordinary power is capable of high attainments outside his own immediate field. But this rule did not apply to Old Hutch. He was a born speculator, one of the most gifted in history, a genius whose sensibilities were tuned to a high key, and one who, in his prime, sensed the course of markets with an accuracy that seemed almost mystic.

Yet when he turned his hand to tasks other than speculation, high success was the invariable reward. Somewhere in him there was the initiative and the vision of the builder. He liked to break new paths, open up new channels of trade, and forge new commercial links. In spite of the irresistible fascination of the speculative markets, which consumed so many years of his life, he found sufficient time to create a number of Chicago institutions and to blaze new trails in the packing industry. In this latter field he held leadership for a long period.

He was unswerving in his early and oft-repeated prediction that Chicago would be the packing center of the world, and when a crowd of strong, vigorous traders flocked to Chicago and launched into the business, Old Hutch joined the procession and soon pushed his way to the front rank.

Long before the city gained its prestige as a packing district, there were livestock markets, but the modern packing center was unknown until the late sixties. It was then that the growing market became the nucleus of one of the greatest manufacturing districts in the world.

When Old Hutch built the first brick packing plant in Chicago, they said it was pride rather than business judgment; that he simply wanted to register his confidence in the future in a concrete way. But the expansion which followed his decision quickly shattered such gossip.

Being a typical old-school packer, he handled nothing but hogs during the winter season. For a decade he held the record in numbers for the entire country. By an unwritten law, the plant handling the largest number of hogs was entitled to display a broom, and for several years this coveted emblem graced the front of the Chicago Packing and Provision company, known as Hutch House.

"Do you see that broom?" Old Hutch used to say

with glowing pride. "Well, let any of these tricky rivals try to take it away and I'll double the capacity by putting in six more killing benches." Each bench was manned by a complete crew which killed and dressed hogs in competition with the others. A fair day's killing was two thousand head.

After the glamour of leadership had lost its lure, after he had set the pace and revelled in the glory of the game, Old Hutch gradually drifted out of the business, for it had always been contrary to his tastes. He had followed it with a tongue-in-the-cheek attitude. But he left a record of achievement. He had succeeded in putting life into the industry, he had sharpened competition, he had paid unprecedented salaries to hog buyers, established an evening provisions exchange, and served as its president. And from the hard school which he conducted there graduated a number of men whose names were to be known far and wide.

At the time it became apparent Old Hutch was quietly withdrawing from the packing business, he was approached by a group of bankers who urged him not only to continue, but to buy up a number of smaller companies and broaden his business enormously, assuring him that there was at his disposal any financial aid that might be needed.

Old Hutch shook his head. "My place," he said, "is in the Wheat Pit. There I find comfort. There I am at rest."

Many of the enterprises which he supported in their infancy became thriving and noteworthy institutions. He organized the Traders Insurance Company and later founded the famous old Corn Exchange Bank. To-day it is merged with the Illinois Merchants Bank, one of the largest in America. Of this project he was justly proud.

In the late sixties desultory warnings were heard that Chicago was inviting a fire catastrophe. With his usual foresight, Old Hutch was among that small group who sensed the growing danger. He had insisted for years that the town was all sham and shingles and could be transformed into a roaring furnace in a twinkling.

Where the solid, towering skyscrapers of Indiana limestone now stud the streets, there were long rows of shells, flimsy shams of stucco, veneer, putty, and pine, topped by roofs of tar and felt. Walls were run up a hundred feet, a single brick in thickness, and heavy wooden cornices skirting the rims were painted gray and buff in imitation of stone. Two thirds of the city's sixty thousand buildings were of wood. It happened, now and then, that one of the fragile shams collapsed.

Cornices were forever toppling of their own weight.

Winds lashing off the inland sea or driving across the prairies from the west were an added hazard. A single spark tossed about in these gales often caused serious mischief. Most of the summer winds were dry and hot, and in the path of the sirocco was a five-mile line of pine buildings. Vast stores of inflammable materials were in open yards or under tar roofs. Old Hutch and other "alarmists" insisted that a long dry season, a driving gale from the southwest, and an exhausted fire department would some day provide the ghastly combination that would sound the city's doom. All these things finally happened.

A blazing sun literally baked the Middlewest and the Northwest during the summer of 1871. Rivers went dry, livestock perished, and ranches burned down, when flying sparks from locomotives fired the dried-out fields. While the West fought this new enemy, a hundred villages went up in smoke, many lives were lost, and refugees poured into the cities from the stricken districts.

Slowly the fires drew toward Chicago, destroying large towns in the lumber districts, including Peshtigo, Wisconsin, where six hundred persons died in the heart of a forest of oaks, pines, and tamaracks.

The drought and withering heat continued into October, and in the first few days of that month thirty fires broke out in Chicago. The merciless rays of a blazing sun, combined with a hot wind, had sucked up every bit of moisture; paint was blistered, and shingles curled up from the heat. Thirty thousand Sunday school children were daily raising their voices in prayer for relief from the drought.

Fear gripped the heart of the city on Saturday night, October seventh, when fire laid flat four entire blocks in two hours. It was a prelude to the onrushing disaster. A planing mill stacked with dry lumber and fluffy with shavings, went up like a puff of powder. A paper box factory passed like a Roman candle. The roaring conflagration was driven forward by a strong south wind. Glowing cinders drifted on the breast of the gale to distant points. Those citizens who did not turn out to help rip down frame shanties in the path of the flames, were busily drenching the roofs of their homes and stamping out firebrands.

All night long and most of the next day the fire boys battled. Late Sunday afternoon they returned to their quarters, victorious but half blinded and exhausted. In less than six hours these civic heroes were to line up again in a battle for the city's life, a battle to be fought with disabled engines, and hose made defective by exposure to flames.

A woman's scream late Sunday night drew attention to the blazing barn of the O'Learys and, incidentally, gave rise to the old canard that the Chicago fire was due to a cow kicking over a lamp held by Mrs. O'Leary, a myth long since disproved. The cause of the fire was never determined.

In a few minutes the doomed city heard the courthouse bell peal out its solemn warning. A wind kicking up from the south quickly veered to the southwest and whipped into a gale. The whole city was lit up by a glare in the western sky. With incredible speed the fire raced toward the river, beyond which lay the heart of the city, its business district. Wooden buildings were licked up like cotton batting.

Then of a sudden a gigantic sheet of flame shot skyward from a match factory. This wall of fire spread under the gale; long red tongues stretched across the river and lapped hungrily at the dry shells fringing the opposite water edge. Planing mills and factories became a line of crimson tubes. A huge grain elevator, roofed and sided with iron, was turned into a tower of fire. Thin iron castings ran molten from the top.

To the horror of frantic crowds that packed the bridges, the wind, growing to high velocity, picked up long banners and streamers of flame and carried them far into the vitals of the city. These glowing pennants spanned the space of the river district with one vaulting leap. Soon brands were shooting about in all directions like incandescent meteors. Almost on the stroke of midnight the earth trembled violently, as the reservoir at the gas works exploded, letting forth a flood of flame that poured out over the city. Chicago's fate was sealed.

Men and women went mad. Mobs packed points of safety, their cries rising to a din, over which could be heard the roar of the gale and the flames, the clang of broken fire engines, and the wail of river vessels with blazing rigging. And mingled in it all was the mournful toll of the courthouse bell.

Old Hutch had driven to the courthouse soon after the conflagration got under way and had placed his employees, himself, and his resources at the disposal of Mayor Mason. With no thought of his own safety he hurried about in the midst of a rain of sparks and firebrands, lending what aid he could to women and children fighting their way through the suffocating streets. He paid hold-up prices to drivers to carry the maimed and injured to the "Purgatory on the Sands," a forty-acre stretch on the lake front to which poor and rich alike fled for safety from the horrors of the inferno.

Exhausted and heavy-hearted, Old Hutch finally withdrew to the edge of the burning district and from a height watched the fascinating splendor of the awful conflagration, unequaled since the burning of Rome. From that vantage point the whole blazing area could be closely observed. There was one large solid mass of fire. Out of this main body there stretched three long fingers of flame, the largest one in the center being flanked by a smaller one on each side. The peculiar formation was startling to observe, for it looked like the lurid foot and talons of an enormous bird of prey. And the crimson talons seemed to be digging deep into the heart of the city. They clutched, receded, clutched again. With every new blast of wind they spread out over a wider and wider area.

The effect of such a calamity as the Chicago fire could not possibly be restricted to the stricken city alone. In the general field of commerce and finance the news would inevitably have a profound influence, at least until the extent of losses to outside interests were definitely determined. Hence the shrewd speculator was quick to sense an opportunity for substantial gain.

As Old Hutch stood upon a roof looking out over the field of ruin and despair, a messenger hurried up the teetering ladder to announce that three excited men were anxious to see him at once on business of most urgent importance. He climbed down to the street level and in the flickering half light recognized the men as traders of some importance on La Salle Street.

"We've been searching the town for you!" blurted one of the men.

"We are forming a pool——"

"Well, what of it?" Old Hutch cut in.

"And we're going to sell hell out of stocks——"

"I'm not interested!"

"And God knows it's a chance in a million. We'll sell rails and industrials and bonds, and bust the market——"

"I want nothing to do with your rotten schemes!" shouted Old Hutch.

"Great God, man, have you lost your reason!" broke in one of the three. "Here's a chance to make millions. A chance in a lifetime. We have wired New York brokers——"

"Get out of my sight!" Old Hutch bellowed in a frenzy of passion. "God damn your filthy souls! You'd trade on the blood of your brothers! With death striking right and left, you think of profit. Out in that roaring furnace babies and womenfolk are being burned to charcoal. And yet you think of profit. To-morrow disease and starvation will begin its toll, and yet you scheme to make filthy money, blood money, gain that comes through the torture and torment of the innocent."

"Out of my sight!" he thundered.

And as the three hurried off, Old Hutch buried his face in his hands and wept, for he loved his Chicago and he loved his calling as a speculator.

"It was the only time in my life," he said many years later, "that I was utterly ashamed of my calling. Only after months could I shake the thought and the cruel picture from my mind. I never could and never did bring myself to trade upon a disaster involving the loss of civilian lives."

No one had dreamed that the fire would eat its way to La Salle Street. But as the night drew on, the flames began their attack upon the splendid line of banking and insurance houses comprising the financial section. Across the bridges and through the black, smoke-filled tunnels under the river business men and employees began racing for the financial section. The suffocating street soon became a Babylon. Iron doors clanked as men fought their way into vaults in an effort to save money and other valuables. Boxes, trunks and baskets were used for carrying out gold, currency, and almost priceless records. Fortunes were tied up in coats and tossed over the shoulder like a knapsack. One banker packed a trunk with a million dollars in greenbacks. When he shouted for an expressman to cart the precious cargo to safety the rate for this work had gone up to a thousand dollars. He gladly paid in advance and began a race for Milwaukee.

Old Hutch had arrived in time to see the beautiful stone Chamber of Commerce building, then occupied by the Wheat Pit, go up in smoke. Substantial structures six stories high were being consumed in five minutes by actual count. The street was transformed into a glowing mass, with red iron columns, twisted fantastically, writhing about in the air like serpents.

Old Hutch saw his Corn Exchange Bank, in which he took such high pride, burn to the street level. But it had been possible to salvage much of the valuables.

And next morning when the sun came up and hung like a crimson ball in the haze of smoke over the lake, one Chicago bank opened for business. It was Old Hutch's bank and it held forth in the basement of his home on Wabash Avenue.

To this day the extent of the losses sustained by Old

Hutch in the Chicago fire is not known. Many believed that his fortune was reduced to a painful point. There could be no doubt that the hand of fate had again fallen heavily upon him. In real estate alone his losses must have been extensive, for his holdings were large and valuable. Insurance companies were driven to the wall, bank records were destroyed in most cases, and property rights were thrown into a muddle by the burning of all courthouse records.

> "Men clasped each other's hands and said
> The city of the West is dead."

Old Hutch gave no evidence of personal loss during that long hideous night in which he continued dispatching telegrams to the outside world for food and medical aid; nor during the following day when he viewed the burned-over prairie city, with its stark and blackened trees scattered about like grim sentinels of death.

Some said he was too shrewd to let his weakened financial position be known. But there were many more who believed his profound grief over the destruction of the city he loved made the loss of his personal fortune shrink into nothingness.

VII

Clash Of Giants

OLD HUTCH again had seen his hopes tossed suddenly into the air and shot to pieces like clay pigeons. His dream had been fading farther and farther into the background and now seemed dim and shadowy. He knew that years of struggle, planning, searching, analyzing and scheming must intervene before he would again be prepared for the gigantic undertaking so close to his heart. If he was discouraged or disheartened he gave no sign, though one of weaker will might well have cried out with Flaubert: "Oh, how often I have fallen back to earth, my nails bleeding, my sides bruised, my head swimming, after having tried to climb straight up this marble wall."

For a long period he remained away from the Wheat Pit. It was gossiped that he had quit for good, that he never again would be a dominating figure, that his old confidence had faded with his losses, and that ambition was dead. Then one day he reappeared. He made no explanations; nor could he be drawn into talk of future plans.

Stick by stick Old Hutch had been rebuilding his house of hope. The spark of genius died down at times, but always burst into flame with each new hope. He was no quitter; he believed in fighting hard, fighting in the open, and to a finish. Soon his power was again being felt, and his star rising anew.

Old Hutch could not be regarded as greedy or avaricious. He wanted money, craved it, but only because money meant power, and power meant an opportunity to unlock the door and plunge headlong into a vast land of dreams.

Not being the flamboyant gambler who would risk all on the turn of a card, he had to move slowly, deliberately toward his goal. He was indeed the very antithesis of such men, for example, as John W. Gates, Bet-you-a-million-Gates, who would lay a thousand dollars on one of two rain drops racing down the window-pane of a pullman car. With a dazzling mind that flew at lightning speed, he was yet the analyst who coldly turned over each problem and weighed it upon the delicate scales of a judicious mind. In those days of fortune building there was always a well thought out plan behind the quick, flashing strokes, strokes that had all the outward appearance of impulse combined with amazing good fortune. He could not go on chance. He had to have sound reason behind each act. Hence the gambler's quicker and more dangerous method of recouping, the method of placing daring and instinct ahead of sound reasoning, found no quarter in the mental processes of Old Hutch. He knew that fortunes were made not by men who entered the market with a preconceived theory as to its immediate course and tried to force that theory, but rather by those who took things as they came, watching the drift, shaping their way from day to day, and, like prudent merchants, going along with the current. It required millions of dollars to force a theory upon a market, and the game was costly if by chance the theory proved wrong.

For the next few years Old Hutch, self-reliant, judicious, and courageous, continued his skillful market drives, slowly, steadily, extending his power. There was no sign of ostentation, no grandiose aping of the melodramatic speculators who had gone before. He was building quietly, soundly, for the day when he might be ready to contend for complete mastery. And that was a task requiring huge sums of money.

From time to time he flashed in and out of the public spotlight, which was forever being trained upon the Wheat Pit. He crossed swords with the leaders one after another. His victories were numerous, his defeats comparatively few. He took his beatings good naturedly enough, even when the victor chanced to be P. D. Armour.

Over a period of years Old Hutch and Armour, a genius of exceptional power, carried on their warfare in the commodity market without letting the feud ever approach the brink of personal hatred. Each man admired the other; each was ready to stand up for the other's commendable traits. And each was forever making it unpleasant for the other, either market-wise or in a personal way.

Old Hutch had a subtle irony. He poked fun at Armour on every possible occasion. Sometimes he succeeded in nettling "Peedy" and thereby felt an enormous glee.

There was the incident of the Honor Park. Loving the uniqueness of Old Hutch and appreciating the things he had done for the city, Chicago offered to name a park after him. It was to be an unusual honor for unusual service. A committee of aldermen with shining jowls, spotless linen, and polished boots, finally waylaid him on the floor of the exchange for the purpose of giving formal notification.

All that day Armour and Hutch had battled for market control, each using his utmost wizardry to trip up the opponent. The day had ended in a draw. When the visiting aldermen surrounded Old Hutch, Armour and his cohorts were merrily on hand.

"Yes," said Old Hutch, "I can use a park, an Honor Park, provided there is a fence around it. . . . What? No fence? . . . Then it is useless to me."

"But the idea ain't to give it to you," broke in one alderman. "It's just an honor, because, you see you're a great citizen. Parks don't have fences. They are places with benches and paths and trees where people can wander free and lazy." Armour and his friends howled with laughter.

"Doesn't sound right to me," persisted Old Hutch. "What I need is a park with a fence. Now you boys go find me one of that kind."

The committee was growing a bit quick tempered. "Say, Mr. B. P. Hutchinson, are you trying to josh us? You know we might hand this here Honor Park along to some one else; we might pass it over to your good friend Peedy Armour?"

"Fine!" shouted Old Hutch. "That's what I've been

thinking. That's why it's no use without a fence. Peedy certainly needs something with honor in it, a park or something. He's the boy we should endow with your honor menagerie. But let's not fool ourselves—there isn't any sort of self-respecting honor in this world that would stick around in a park five minutes with Peedy unless it was tight-fenced in."

The crowd roared. Armour grumbled for a moment, and then joined in the laughter.

"I always knew Ben Hutchinson was a greater stage wit than speculator," was Armour's barbed comment.

There was a curious similarity about the two men. Both hated pretense, hypocrisy, extravagance, untruth, and tyranny, although both were at times branded as tyrants. Neither was ever guilty of welching. Nor did their most persistent enemies accuse them of double-dealing. Both had bodies of iron, sturdy wills, and solemnly believed that work never had and never would hurt any one.

Armour, like Old Hutch, was born on a farm and started making his own way at an early age. In the winter of 1852 he joined three other boys and struck out on a long trek west in the mad rush for gold. Rumor had it that he made the trip neither for lust of gold nor love of excitement, but because a narrow-minded school master had chastised and humiliated him for taking an innocent ride with a beautiful classmate.

At any rate, with a pack on his back, young Armour faced toward the land of Eldorado and walked the entire distance from New York state in six months. One companion died on the way, and the two others turned back, but Armour never thought of giving up. He was like that.

On his arrival he began making money, not by digging California gold, but by digging ditches. His payroll grew from one man to several hundred before finally he started back east to take up grain and packing and lay the foundations of one of the world's largest industries.

"Idleness!" Armour used to say. "I hate the word itself. Rich or poor, there is no more vicious man in any community than the one who is voluntarily idle."

Extravagance or waste was to him the next greatest sin. His distaste was typified in the incident of the dress suit.

A certain young man in the Armour employ had earned P. D.'s approval and was informed that at Christmas time he would be rewarded. It was somewhat of a disappointment to him, therefore, when Christmas came, to receive not an increase in pay but an order on a tailor for a suit of clothes. He was not in need of business clothes and more or less at a loss to know what to do with the order until the idea of a dress suit struck him.

The slip mentioned no figures, and the tailor had his order to go ahead, and so he did to the best of his abilities. The bill was rendered to P. D. He looked at it for several moments before calling the youth in. Then gazing at him sternly, he said, "Young man, I have been slaughtering hogs for forty years—" "Yes Sir"—"But," continued P. D., "to the best of my knowledge this is the first time I ever dressed one."

He had no patience with late sleepers. He arose at five o'clock, breakfasted with his wife by candle light, walked into the city, and had things humming at the office by seven. He remained at his desk until six at night, with but a short respite at noon. By the mid-nineties, besides his huge packing interests, he was owner of an elevator system that included those along two railroads, with a twelve million bushel capacity, then the largest in the world; he owned five thousand railroad cars, a fleet of lake vessels, and helped direct a bank and a railroad.

Armour was easily the most worthy and at the same time the most dangerous single rival with whom Old

Hutch ever matched wits. And yet his natural market skill and generalship never approached that of Hutch. He took the lead in numerous big deals. And almost invariably Old Hutch, who seemed to be standing on the sidelines, came out a winner. He had been slipping in and out of the market, anticipating the moves of Armour and his associates, and profiting both on the rise and on the fall.

In 1878 Armour headed a large bull clique. He manipulated the Chicago and Milwaukee markets. By engineering a corner in a certain grade of wheat he sent the price ten cents over another grade of superior quality.

Many millers who were short wheat held off until the expiration of the temporary corner, expecting the usual break in prices. But Armour was too shrewd for this. He held tight all of that particular grade of spring wheat. To keep running, the millers were finally forced to pay him a high, artificial price. Armour's profits topped the million dollar mark on this one deal.

"Did you take part, Mr. Hutchinson?" a friend asked.

"Well, I must confess that Peedy Armour does me a good turn now and then. Perhaps this one was so intended."

Armour switched about from wheat to corn and from corn to provisions. There would be long periods when he remained out of the market. Sometimes it was due to disturbances which kept him hustling at the stock yards, such as that in 1886, when his life was in danger, and there were persistent reports of attempts to poison him.

After that flurry subsided, he returned to the market with the comment that he craved excitement. "Things are getting dead out at the yards."

He decided to bull the market for pork. Starting in January he forced the price up gradually, arousing little excitement. An echo of labor strife helped his cause, as did also a small crop of hogs. He forced May pork higher and higher, the price rising fifty per cent in two months. Even then the agents of the manipulator refused to let go of any quantity. By the end of the month the price was still sky-rocketing; the shorts were in a vise, and Armour was tightening the screws.

Finally the shorts began shipping in pork from Boston to fill their contracts, and the price tumbled rapidly.

Four million dollars in four months was the reported clean-up of Mr. Armour on this single deal. "A million a month!" groaned the shorts.

At that particular time Armour and Old Hutch were none too friendly, and certainly the latter had no official part in the deal. But again he must have touched a good dividend, judging from a brief press notice which said simply:

"News that Mr. B. P. Hutchinson had also profited handsomely came as a complete surprise."

In one other instance Old Hutch went into the provisions market on a tremendous scale. It was when Peter McGeogh of Milwaukee made his debut—and his departure—as a speculative king.

McGeogh had visions such as frequently troubled many others. He felt that the hour had arrived, that the conditions were precisely right, and that his own judgment was faultless. So he ran a big corner in lard in 1883. And it smashed him financially.

When the crash came, Old Hutch stepped into the market with his millions and saved the situation. The peculiar conditions made his position unique; he had it within his means to grind a number of firms between the rocks of financial ruin and himself profit as a result. Among them were several of his most persistent enemies. Instead he risked his own money to right the situation, prevented a panic on the Street, and quit with a moderate profit for the service he performed. It was one of several acts that endeared Old Hutch to the heart of financial Chicago.

Corners in grain have almost invariably resulted in disastrous failures. The reason is simple. The volume of products is large. There are too many sources of supply to permit of a monopoly. This was true even as far back as half a century ago. At that time when news of an attempted corner stormed the country farmers began sweeping their bins. As prices rose, new wheat poured in from a thousand and one unsuspected sources. The volume of such wheat was always an unknown quantity. Usually it flowed to market like a river that could not be dammed by the puny hands of the manipulator.

Manipulation is a game of millions. A man of limited means, or even a man of moderate wealth, cannot indulge in it. He is beaten at the start. The manipulator must be in command of immense resources with freedom to use such finances at will.

James R. Keene long held a unique place in the stock market as a skillful manager of colossal operations for himself and for syndicates. As a man of wealth and as the agent of capitalists he wielded an enormous power.

In stocks as in politics, the manipulator stays in the

background and pulls the wires. By a scientific arrangement of his forces, as intricate and fascinating as a game of chess, the stock manipulator, particularly in the old days, was able to overthrow normal influences and thus establish desired prices. But even in those times of feeble, flexible rules of discipline the stock manipulator had to be wily enough to avoid going too far from the true basis of value, otherwise he would be overwhelmed. Knowing the precise limit was the mark of genius. Keene knew these boundary lines in stocks just as Old Hutch knew them in wheat.

Cornering stocks is much less difficult than cornering grain. There is really no comparison. In stocks one does not have the "unknown quantity" to struggle with. The manipulator of stocks knows the number of shares out, usually he knows where they are held and how strongly they are held. Moreover, he is enabled to establish other salient facts about which the grain manipulator can only conjecture

It often happened that successful stock operators would decide to turn to the grain markets. Many of them paid a high price for their folly. Keene's lesson took a heavy toll. He had dreamed of cornering the market for corn. His attempt failed utterly. His losses ran high.

Again Keene sought the crown of Wheat King. His great deal extended over a period of nearly a year. In line with his usual course Keene organized a pool and began activity in the autumn of 1878. Five million dollars was the initial sum placed at his disposal by the clique, with another five million in the offing to be used when and if it became necessary. Five million dollars was not a large sum with which to seek control of the wheat market even a half century ago.

During the following winter months the Keene deal was the big market sensation and overshadowed everything else. Most of the supply of actual wheat in Chicago had been gobbled up early in the campaign. The deal was progressing satisfactorily when, on March seventh, the Chicago brokers for Keene received a telegram bearing his name which ordered them to sell his holdings at a certain price. The brokers at once dumped nearly three million bushels of wheat on the market. Under the avalanche of selling the price broke six cents in a short time.

A wire was sent to Keene advising him of the sales and asking for further instructions. Keene was stunned by the message, for he had given no instructions to sell his holdings. He so advised his brokers, who, in a panic over the blunder due to a bogus message, rushed into the market and bought the wheat back.

The source of the bogus telegram is still one of the dark mysteries of the Wheat Pit. Certainly Old Hutch never stooped to such trickery. But his profits incident to the wide swings were reported to be substantial.

The finger of suspicion was pointed to Keene. He was accused of having trumped up the bogus message scheme for the purpose of drawing into the market a large number of speculators who were suspicious of the whole situation. His reply to these charges was prompt and definite. He offered a reward of twenty-five thousand dollars to anyone having information that might lead to the identity of the one who had forged the message.

Keene had reinstated the most of his wheat. Reports from Europe indicated a larger demand for our surplus. With this in mind he formed the design of extending his original program. In a very short time he had purchased eleven million additional bushels of wheat in the futures market. The five million dollars of emergency money was tossed into the hopper. And Keene soon learned that there was more wheat in the country than he had anticipated and that Old Hutch was among those who kept pouring wheat down upon his back, wheat which he was forced to accept in order not to burst the ever-swelling bubble. His sleep was disturbed and his health endangered by the enormous strain. A financial poet of the time attained some note by his widely quoted "Song of Wheat" dedicated to Keene's unhappy predicament. Perhaps chief merit lay in timeliness rather than poetical art:

> "With mind distracted and worn,
>   With eyelids heavy and red,
> Jim Keene lay in canopied state,
>   Rolling and tossing in bed,
> Checks, Checks, Checks!
>   On every bank in the street,
> And still with a voice of dolorous pitch,
>   Would that its tones could reach the rich,
> Hutch, and Dow, and Kent, and sich,
>   He sang this Song of the Wheat."

Keene finally did overcome the major obstacles and maintained a price sufficiently high to squeeze a million dollars out of the shorts. At that time, however, it is understood that Old Hutch had taken the long side. And it is not impossible that he profited to a far greater extent than did the Keene clique, for after they had paid all costs of operation and divided the comparatively small profits, there was not enough left to regard the manipulation as a success. General conditions favored the manipulator. Otherwise the losses would have been disastrous.

After weighing all factors, the large sums involved, the innumerable stumbling blocks encountered, the long sleepless nights that followed days of margin calls, Mr. Keene was satisfied to relinquish his claims to leadership in the Wheat Pit. He returned to the easier and more profitable pastime of stock manipulation.

"I am turning the Pit back to Old Hutch," was Keene's sarcastic comment.

Since it is not intended in this narrative to attempt chronological accuracy, but rather to present a picture of the stormiest periods of Wheat Pit history, and the exploits of its most remarkable and picturesque character, many of the minor drives, squeezes, and temporary corners manipulated by Old Hutch must necessarily be eliminated.

In the ten years following the Chicago fire, his successes were many, and his fortune continued piling higher and higher. Often the attempted corner of some other plunger was turned to his own advantage by sheer speculative skill. Under the lashing flame of his genius many situations which threatened dire results to his own fortune were somehow strangely transformed into events of much rejoicing.

By the mid-eighties he was a financial giant, prepared to risk all in one swift dramatic attempt to do
what had been called the impossible. From then on he
simply bided his time until all signs should point to
success, "until even the stars in the sky blinked their
approval." Then he struck, struck hard, with lightning
swiftness and deadly accuracy.

VIII

Crazy Harper

MEN take a curious pride in power. They like to feel important, to be pointed out. Desire for power becomes an obsession. Rosy dreams of conquest swallow up thoughts of danger. Like a soulless siren, the promise of power beckons many into deeper and blacker waters where only the most skillful survive.

For attaining quick power and world fame, the Wheat Pit has always proved a fascinating lure. Often enough it has been said that the average speculator would rather be undisputed Wheat King than be the ruling monarch of a nation. Perhaps that is an exaggeration. But it has some basis in fact. The long list of men who have trailed their golden dreams over the brink of ruin bears witness to how the prize is coveted.

In the hectic scramble for Wheat Pit leadership some

men have lost only their fortunes. Others have lost their good standing in the community, along with the fortunes of those who believed in them. Crazy Harper paid the price with his life.

Little was known of the boyhood and youth of E. L. Harper. He had been a sewing machine agent before he engaged in the pig iron business, and long before he became a banker. He was a dominating character, and his persuasive powers must have been immense. As a sewing machine agent his prosperity was rather remarkable, and stories of his prowess include a large wager that he could sell sewing machines to the savages of the South Sea Islands. No one had courage to cover the bet.

Harper was credited with being able to sell more sewing machines in a miserly district than three men could sell in a given time in the most prosperous district. He would bet even money that in thirty minutes he could sell a machine in any home selected on a residence street. And he seldom lost.

His sales tricks were as varied as they were numerous. The most "flashy" sale was clinched with hardly a word. In his pompous, impressive way Harper would ask for the lady of the house, and present his gaudy card. Then he would lean forward and whisper:

"Can you keep a secret?"

"Why, certainly."

Snatching out a pad of paper and a pencil he would jot down a list of figures. They included such items as dressmaker's discount, salesman's commission, cash discount, advertising discount, and the like. Then he would rapidly total the items and appear to subtract them from the regular sale price of the machine.

"Quick!" he would say. "If you are a woman of decision act now or forever lose a golden opportunity."

To prevent the "amazing bargain" from slipping away the woman usually acted hastily. If she showed a slight tendency to hesitate, Harper offered other apparent price inducements that clamped the deal.

His greatest pride was in selling two machines to a home, if it chanced to be a two-story house, one for the upstairs and one for the main floor. No woman should kill herself climbing up and down. It was the duty of a loving husband to protect her health.

"Most any chump can sell a machine in a prosperous American home. But it takes skill to sell two to a family." Such was his proud boast.

Harper had skill. He had daring; perhaps too much. He developed exceptional business sagacity. And having found favor with certain business leaders in Cincinnati he was lifted almost overnight into the field of banking, where he finally became vice president of the Fidelity National Bank, which occupied the most imposing building in that city.

It was while holding this post in 1887 that Harper conducted his mad crusade against the market in the hope of snatching the crown of Wheat King. Incidentally, he blocked for one year the big scheme of Old Hutch, but this proved fortunate for the latter, as the subsequent year offered more attractive natural conditions.

In a quiet sort of way, Harper had dabbled with the wheat market for several years. Few of his intimates knew of these speculations. None of them knew that in the two preceding years he had met with rather marked success. It was this taste of victory that induced him to try the vicious raid.

Mystery veiled the activity of the Pit for nearly half of the year, or until after the bursting of the Harper intrigue. Then it developed that not one, but several groups had secretly schemed to corner the market during a period of six months.

The first group, which became known as the California Syndicate, launched its under-cover campaign at the beginning of the year. A member of this syndicate had returned from Europe with indisputable information of a crop shortage which should eventually send American wheat prices skyward. A hook-up had been made with a group in the Liverpool market. By an unfortunate turn, however, this latter group had been bearish and was short much wheat, sold at lower prices. So there was some delay in starting the bull market, for the erstwhile English bears, now converted bulls, were reluctant to accept their painful losses.

This they did, however, and then proceeded to buy up the available wheat in Liverpool, at the same time controlling the shipments from the western coast.

Meantime a group of Chicago bears had laid plans for a campaign. With quick strokes they attacked the market and drove prices downward. The California Syndicate soon faced a loss of ten cents a bushel on millions of bushels of wheat. But instead of becoming panic stricken they continued buying at the lower prices until the average loss was only a few cents a bushel. It developed into a tug of war between powerful factions, each group having large sums at its disposal. The bears finally found themselves in a trap. May wheat soared, and they were forced to take their losses and withdraw from the fray.

Profits for the California Syndicate would have run

into dazzling figures had not other secret forces crept into the drama with the firm determination to give the Californians a taste of their own medicine. Something happened in the banks that prevented the westerners from obtaining the funds they had expected, with which to take in all the May wheat. Prices collapsed. The deal ended without profit to those who had sought to rig the market. The leaders of the California Syndicate slipped quietly away from the fray and took their punishment in silence. Another great "corner" had flattened out into failure.

Just then a new and powerful influence began to dominate the market. Here again deep mystery shrouded every move. Early in May rumor credited the westerners with having entered into a truce with their former antagonists for the purpose of cornering June wheat. But this was sheer rumor.

Professional traders have always despised attempted corners. A tight squeeze was apt to break a good many people. It violently unsettled values. The Pit became as dangerous as a powder mine. To the broker and trader, a corner was what a cyclone is to a farmer who wants only a shower. So at the first hint of a corner, the trade was always ready to put on its war paint. Various factions would forget differences and solidify against the common enemy, the man or group attempting the corner.

But in this case it was difficult to ferret out the brains of the big deal. Finally there came a report that a Cincinnati clique was the cause of the upheaval and that fifty million bushels of wheat for June delivery had been purchased. On the heels of this rumor came another which pointed a strong finger at the Fidelity National Bank, the Harper bank. This brought a blunt and indignant denial from officers.

The purchases of wheat went on. A thousand carloads a day were poured into the city. Warehouses were choked. Railroad sidings were full of laden cars waiting for some place to unload. Still the "mysterious clique" bought. It seemed to have endless resources.

New rumors flew about. Reports had it that J. W. Mackay and his bonanza king friends, who had been linked with the California Syndicate, were now in control. Later it was the Standard Oil millionaires. Still later it was an alliance of banks directed from Wall Street. Finally all suspicion again was centered upon Cincinnati, but no one dreamed that Harper was playing a lone hand and had tossed all of life's chips on the table in one flashing gamble for world fame. No one dreamed that Harper himself was starting all the rumors as a screen to his plan.

The air became tense. Trained speculators knew a tornado was brewing. In the big speculative markets there are always men fearless enough to challenge a contender. Harper had created what seemed to be a formidable situation. But two men were determined to match strength with what was believed to be a strong clique. They were Nat Jones and Norman B. Ream. Without warning they suddenly raided the market, selling millions of bushels for June delivery. Harper held firm until the wicked price slump began cutting into him. Then he let go of fifteen million bushels. Prices had another sharp break. But Harper was not without courage. Somehow he obtained more money and bought back the fifteen million bushels and many millions more at the lower price. His victory now seemed assured.

He had not accurately counted the enemy, however, nor had he realized that the first blow was simply a test of the market.

When the gong sounded for the opening of business on Monday, June thirteenth, the second and heavier blow was struck. In a jiffy prices tumbled five cents.

And the bears realized at last that the supposed clique was not omnipotent. Harper seemed a bit dazed by the recurring blows. He was glad for the truce which prevailed on Monday on the rumor that a Cincinnati man was en route to Chicago with a "pot of gold" to rout the bears.

Early Monday night Harper's brokers met behind closed doors at the old Richelieu Hotel. Lights blazed high in the room throughout the long night. The meeting was being closely watched.

In the cold gray dawn a little group of men stepped from the hotel. They tried to appear at ease. But the deep lines of trouble marking each face, and the quick jerky movements betrayed their predicament to the skilled market observers. With a pitiful show of nonchalance questioners were waved aside, and the conferees set off for their respective brokerage offices.

Defeat was in the air. That queer, tense stillness that pervades the vast trading floor just prior to big market explosions had fallen like a velvet curtain. The Pit filled a few minutes earlier than usual. Brokers were silent. The early morning fun was forgotten. Each man had an expectant, half-frightened look.

At the first boom of the gong bedlam broke loose. The bears rushed upon the Harper brokers like mad men.

They were selling wheat, millions of bushels, while prices crashed downward. Harper's brokers slowly fought their way up from the center of the teeming ring of traders. They pawed through the crowd to the rim of the Pit where they stood for a moment in sort of a daze, gasping for air, swaying slightly from side to side, and waiting for new instructions from Harper. These came in an instant:

"Sell it all quick!"

Down into the center of the Pit they leaped. Their nimble fingers began writing in the air—writing new low prices at which Harper, the man who would be Wheat King, was selling his wares, his hopes, and his life.

First it was a rout. Then it became a panic. In two hours wheat had dropped nineteen cents a bushel.

By noon the battle had died down to a low painful murmur.

At that hour the secretary of the exchange stepped briskly out upon the little south balcony overlooking the trading floor. Everyone knew what his appearance meant. Instantly all activity ceased, and a dead silence prevailed. A few men walked off to the side of the hall, dreading to hear the news. Several others appeared on the verge of collapse and were supported by companions.

In a strong clear voice the secretary began reading a list of names of certain firms holding membership on the exchange. There were nineteen companies in all. Before he had finished reading a few men here and there were seen to dash out of the hall. When the list was completed the secretary added these crushing words:

"All of the foregoing firms have failed."

So the Harper debacle had wrecked nineteen houses on the street. These companies had been directly or indirectly drawn into the vacuum created by his immense dealings.

But the news that electrified the business world was to come a day later. It took the form of an announcement that the "mysterious clique" was a single man— E. L. Harper. And it added that he had looted the Fidelity National Bank of its last available dollar to carry on his quixotic scheme. Thousands of small depositors saw their savings of a lifetime snatched from them in a twinkling. The bank's assets had been seven million dollars.

Crazy Harper, broken and dejected, shorn of that persuasive power that had made him stand out among men, submitted to arrest with hardly a word. The look of pain and terror that came over him when he realized he had brought about one of the greatest financial catastrophes in the history of grain speculation, still marked his features months after the prison doors had clanked, and he had begun his ten-year sentence.

It was while serving this term in the Ohio state prison that details of his tragic campaign were revealed.

Before he began stealing the funds of the bank Harper had fed his own fortune of two or three million into the Wheat Pit. The feat he had intended seemed to grow larger and larger as he proceeded. Every few days it would appear that an additional hundred thousand dollars would bridge the gap. The goal looked too close, too tempting, to think of turning back.

This is the method Harper devised for stealing the funds of the bank. One of his brokers, or one of the several corporations which he controlled, would give a check on the Fidelity bank or some other bank. But this check would not be charged up to the account against which it was drawn, or if on another bank, it would not be forwarded for collection. Instead, the teller of the Fidelity, under Harper's orders, would hold it and count it as cash. These bogus cash items mounted steadily during the campaign until they reached staggering totals. They were straining the very life of the bank for weeks before the crash came.

"Didn't you ever mention these items to other directors?" Harper was asked.

For a moment he stared in amazement. Then, "Good God, no! Those figures were like ghosts that haunted me at night. They kept me awake until I thought I should be driven mad. In the day time they were like corpses, a long line of corpses that no one has the courage to approach. Some days I would muster strength to glance at the teller's scratches. And there were times when I longed to look at the items themselves; that seemed the sensible thing to do. But I didn't look because"——

Harper paused in his statement and, on being urged to continue, he added: "I didn't look at the figures because deep in my heart I knew that one look would strike me cold. I knew I would be permanently paralyzed."

When all the wreckage had been cleared away and Harper sent off to prison, the market analysts discovered that fate had played a grim trick upon the ambitious sewing machine agent. For had he been able to raise another half million dollars, his plan likely would have netted him millions of dollars profit. But this thought was of little solace to Harper. He was the type of man who wants first prize or none. He wanted to be Wheat King, with the world pointing to him as the wizard who single-handed had conquered the field. Instead he spent his days mooning behind prison bars, planning and replanning his campaign, and dreaming of another chance. He would never make the same mistakes, he used to say. He had paid for his schooling, and now was confident of success. All he needed was another chance; all he lived for was another chance.

One day, as Harper was seated in his favorite chair in the prison reading room, staring off into space, the warden approached with brisk step. He was smiling broadly, and in his hand he held a large white envelope. Harper knew at a glance that the long delayed pardon had come at last, and that once more he was a free man. There was no show of emotion on his part as the warden confirmed his suspicions. In a formal sort of way he thanked the warden for his kindness, then packed up his few belongings and departed. He went back home and died. The Wheat Pit had at last taken its full toll.

Harper's death was not unexpected. From the very hour of his crushing defeat, he had been a poor wreck, physically and mentally, a weakling who failed to respond to the puny efforts of skilled physicians, and whose days were numbered. He had put too much into the battle.

Harper died and was forgotten. Save for the boisterous clank of his battle-armor over a period of forty days, he was to the Wheat Pit only a genealogical incident. But he is still remembered by many whom he ruined. His only glory, if it may be called glory, was to win a permanent niche in the speculative hall of fame by reason of having strewn financial wreckage across half a dozen states.

Old Hutch was a fascinated spectator of the Harper fiasco. He must have sensed from the very start that a single man, rather than a clique, was directing the campaign. Shortly after the Harper drive began to churn the market and cause price gyrations, a group of brokers encountered Old Hutch on the trading floor. He was in a friendly, talkative mood.

"Mr. Hutchinson," one of them asked, "in your opinion what interests are back of this campaign?"

Old Hutch thought for a moment, and then replied:

"There are no 'interests,' unless one man may be called an interest. When the smoke clears away and the wreckage is drawn from the tracks, you will find that one man is the brains, and the stupidity, of the deal. And quite likely you will find that the poor fellow is crazy. No sane man would follow such tactics. No sane man would consider himself bigger than this world market."

Yet at the very time Old Hutch made the comment he was himself standing on the threshold of his historic crusade. He was waiting only for the hour to strike. Then he meant to prove that the man could indeed be bigger than the market if blessed with the peculiar genius that creates speculative heroes, or villains, depending upon the point of view. Throughout the Harper affair he had eyed every change with marked intensity. He was like a master surgeon watching the lean blade wielded by a less skilled surgeon bending over his subject in a dissecting room. Each slight variation of the shiny steel in its downward stroke carried a meaning to the master.

How much Old Hutch learned from studying the Harper deal will never be known. Certainly he was no less courageous by the gigantic failure. On the contrary, there were those who contended that it gave him greater confidence.

At any rate, he let the remaining months of the year roll away without indicating the slightest interest in the market. Then the hour arrived, and Old Hutch began to make history. . . .

IX

The Trap

LIKE a thunder-bolt he struck. The market quivered. Then it stiffened and became calm. Once more Old Hutch aimed a mighty blow. The market shook like an injured beast, staggered, and collapsed. A deluge of selling orders flooded the Pit. In the wild panic, seasoned brokers tossed their wares overboard at crumbling prices. Wheat Pit history holds no more breathless moment.

Old Hutch was in the heat of his campaign. He had timed his drive to the hour. Now he seemed to be everywhere at once, scrutinizing every new movement. As he strode across the trading floor, his flashing eye took in each detail of wreckage, while his tall gaunt frame towering six and a half feet, struck terror in the hearts of hardy plungers. He snapped out orders to a dozen brokers and watched the executions with the eagerness of a circus manager driving his flunkies to a quick opening after a storm.

He was an imposing figure, this old man who dreamed of dictating bread prices. Over his great frame, straight as a steel rod, was draped the same ancient square-cut clothes in vogue many years before; the suit was a criss-cross between the cutaway, the sack, and the frock. He buttoned the faded black coat only at the top, and the ends flapped about loosely as he walked, giving much the appearance of an exaggerated scarecrow. The old fashioned high collar was protected by a loose neckerchief of a garish crimson, and the black felt hat had a broad rakish brim that was forever swaying about and taking on new lines and new shapes.

Every time the market would begin to steady, the deep throated calls of Old Hutch could be heard above the din.

"Give them another fifty, Billy!" Or, "Sell them another hundred, Tom!"

Hutch was pounding prices down, down, down; it was a part of his scheme of domination. He knew that one who corners the market must clear away the prevailing supplies at low figures, and he prepared to absorb the invisible surplus that later pours in from undreamed of sources. For the time Hutch wanted low prices and was out to get them.

It was shortly after the first of the year, 1888, that his hammering process began. His son, the late Charles L. Hutchinson, banker, philanthropist, and famous patron of art, had just been elected president of the Board of Trade after a heated campaign which had angered Old Hutch by reason of remarks by the opposition reflecting upon his own conduct.

"Son," he was quoted as saying, "I want you to accept this nomination. You'll win the presidency because the city believes in you and this board of trade believes in you. And here's one thing more to remember. Your own dad believes still more in you. And in trading in this market I'll not only follow the rules of the board, but I'll also abide by your own wishes in any problems that may arise."

"Do you mean that, father?" asked young Hutchinson. "I've never known you to go back on your word."

"Of course I mean it, son." And Old Hutch clinched the pledge by throwing his arm about the young man's shoulder and drawing him close, little realizing what tremendous bearing the pledge would have upon his future course.

It was a warm campaign for the presidency of the

Wheat Pit, a campaign in which the Chicago papers took a lively part. They strongly defended the good character of Old Hutch. They quoted prominent business men who came forward to eulogize him for saving many Chicago firms in times of panic.

"And I'm not sure but that he and his bank did not save the city itself not so long ago," one man was quoted in the *Tribune* as saying. "The old man stood like a rock when other bankers were wringing their hands and flopping about like headless chickens." He was credited, too, with having prevented "A panic of dreadful proportions" when the Harper bubble burst. It was the first time that this news had come out, and more praise was heaped upon Old Hutch.

Thus did the city again extend its assurance of high esteem to the old man of the Pit. And his boy, Charlie, was elected to the high and coveted office by a vote of five to one.

Meantime, with his sledge-hammer blows, Old Hutch continued thumping the market throughout the first two months of the year. He would sell, sell, sell, until prices seemed to scrape bottom. Then he would buy back what he had sold, absorbing it through skillfully scattered sources, and in addition he would each time add somewhat to the holdings of wheat he meant to retain. He was selling the market down quickly, buying back at lower prices what he had sold, taking his profits, and purchasing wheat to be removed from the market. Over and over he repeated the operation, until the Pit became genuinely alarmed. It was plain that he had launched more than a temporary campaign. It was plain, too, that he could not be stopped. How much money he had with which to finance the biggest deal ever attempted was not known and to this day is not known. But it was reported in 1881 that his personal fortune was twenty million dollars, and in the subsequent seven years he had been quite prosperous.

Now he was watching the market as he had never watched it before. From gong to gong he observed every fraction of price variation. After the final bell of the session he would go over to the famous old Century Club, hard by, where he was lord and master, and where he sometimes stirred a kettle of soup for his cronies as he made or unmade world market conditions.

One day as he was leaving the Pit after having administered one of his daily drubbings, half a thousand brokers burst into song:

> "I see Old Hutch start for his club
> Goodbye, my money, goodbye,
> He's given us all a terrible rub
> Goodbye, my money, goodbye."

Old Hutch was extremely annoyed by the affront. He suspected his ancient friendly enemy, P. D. Armour, of having inspired the bit of distasteful raillery. Perhaps he let P. D. know his suspicions. At any rate the old clash was renewed, Armour taking the opposite side of the market. He battered away at Hutch without making the slightest impression and then, for the first time, it was realized with pain and chagrin that Old Hutch *was* the market.

"The one man power," said the daily press, "was never exhibited more forcibly." Sensing what was in the wind, a few long-headed men began predicting that Old Hutch would become the permanent dictator of world wheat prices.

Perhaps these very rumors helped to solidify the forces against him. For it was not long until Edward Partridge, notorious bear, had turned bull with Armour to help crush the dominance of Old Hutch. The answer of the old man was a standing offer to sell as much oats in the market as was desired at a certain fixed price, and another offer to buy any quantity "up to the entire crop" at a slightly lower price. In other words he declared his complete rulership over oats by fixing the prices in which they might be traded. It was a daring move at that time, for it was an open challenge to the field.

And the field responded to the challenge. The widely dreaded big four—Cudahy, Ream, Nat Jones and Linn —who were a powerful market factor, jumped into the fray against Hutch, and predictions began to fly that the old man would go the way of the Harpers, the Keenes, and the McGeoghs. Such odds as he now faced were too great for a single warrior.

Hutch seemed unperturbed, however, and proceeded to blaze away with still greater force. Firms that opposed him were lashed into submission or, like the old house of Bensley Brothers, driven to the wall and removed from the field of combat.

A strike of rail engineers at a critical time tended to aid Hutch in his scheme of price demoralization. But more significant factors worked against him. There was, for instance, the sharp market upheaval on the reported death of Emperor William of Germany. Then came certain warlike moves on the part of Russia. This latter disturbance sent prices soaring for a day or two, making things unpleasant for Old Hutch, but at the same time serving one important purpose. Moses Fraley, the big St. Louis plunger, who was forever getting tangled up in the boats of Old Hutch, was at last caught in the flurry and crushed completely, his losses in a twinkling mounting to a million dollars. He was definitely counted out, and, like the good sport he was, he stepped aside without a whimper.

During the second week of May somewhat of a sensation was created by publication of the government's crop report, setting forth a gloomy prospect. Now at last the Big Four, and the other protagonists, Armour, Partridge, and their associates, thought they had Old Hutch with his back to the wall. Prices shot upward by reason of their immense purchases. They chuckled and chortled at the suspected predicament of their enemy. But once again they were wrong. The Old Man, as usual, had thought ahead of the crowd. He had sensed danger and had swung to the bull side. So the efforts of his opponents were simply adding to his profits.

When he decided the advance had gone far enough, the shrewd old man turned about once more and again battered the aching sides of the Pit. He kept the market in a turmoil, administering chastisement here and there and forcing many of his opponents to withdraw, one by one, from the field of battle.

At the end of a particularly nerve-wracking day some one from the camp of the Big Four called out a

doleful warning that Hutch would at length meet a
worse fate than the gentleman of the Mouse Tower on
the Rhine "who was devoured by rodents for cornering
grain in time of famine."

Old Hutch laughed outright.

"Now the trouble with you boys," he said, striding
over to the group, "the trouble is that you know speculation only just about as well as you know your history.

"It is pure legend that Hatto II, Bishop of Mainz,
was punished by a plague of rodents for cornering
grain.

"The silly tale is a corruption of various medieval
traditions. Hatto II, so far as is known, was a generous,
kindly person, although it is said his predecessor Hatto
I, was thrown alive by the devil into the crater of
Mount Etna. At first the story ran that it was Count
Groff who hoarded all the wheat in a year of famine,
and that rats invaded his granary, consumed the grain,
and, overrunning the tower, devoured the count himself. Another legend is to the effect that Widerolf,
Bishop of Strassburg, was destroyed by mice because
he suppressed the convent of Selzen in 997.

"All of these originally independent and unbeautiful
tales were eventually tacked onto poor Hatto II, probably because it was he who constructed the Mausheturm

(toll tower) near Bingen on the Rhine. The name of this tower was gradually corrupted to Mauseturm (mouse tower).

"Now, boys, I mention these facts simply by way of showing how easy it is to be wrong in one's conclusions. I suggest that you fellows read history and mythology for a time and leave the wheat market alone.

"In passing I might add that you have had adequate time to get out of the market, or to keep right with the market, and when things get going lively like, I don't want any of you weeping on my shoulder. I'm going to do a lot of things before the mice eat me, and some of them won't please you chaps."

That was the old man's warning, that and nothing more. To those of a judicious turn it was sufficient. They revised their market views and allowed him a wide berth. But the stubborn leaders of the Pit were determined to go on waging battle, and for this they eventually paid aplenty.

By the sixth day of July Old Hutch was credited in the nation's press with having piled up a greater fortune in half a year than he had ever before acquired.

By the tenth day of July he had chartered vessels and was moving grain to the seaboard as a means of tightening his grip on supplies. Smaller markets scattered through America were feeling the pinch of his iron heel. Already he had begun toying with foreign markets, buying and selling on an enormous scale through various secret forces and keeping European prices in line with the trend in the United States.

Slowly, doggedly, he was climbing toward complete mastery. Slowly, quietly, he was closing his agonizing trap upon the bears. Some of his erstwhile enemies were liberal enough to concede his apparent victory, while a large portion of the press bluntly referred to him as the new market dictator, the "Napoleon of Wheat." Such was the state of affairs on the tenth day of July.

And on the very next day came the historic fall of Old Hutch.

X

Iron Stairs

OLD HUTCH is dead!

The startling news went ringing up and down La Salle street that hot stuffy morning in July, 1888, and caused a flurry of excitement. The report descended upon the Pit like a typhoon. Bulls and bears alike regarded the event as one of incalculable importance. At once they began wondering whether the immense holdings of the dictator would be dumped upon the market and crush prices to new low levels. Perhaps some other man of genius would step forward to carry on the task of the market master.

After a short pause, a frenzy of buying and selling ensued. Then there was utter calm. The ghost of Old Hutch seemed to hover over the Pit and point that long sinister forefinger of doom at those who dared to trade on the reported tragedy. A dozen courageous plungers at length gathered just over the rim of the

Pit and held long and earnest consultation. Then they rushed into the center of the ring and began selling, not thousands, but millions of bushels of wheat. Prices sagged sharply under the weight of the offerings.

But this scheme came to a quick death, for two of the plungers observed that the wheat they were selling was passing directly into the hands of shrewd brokers in the employ of Old Hutch. Every bushel had been snapped up by these able emissaries. Here indeed was a new puzzle for the Pit.

Its solution came in good season and took the form of a message from Old Hutch himself. One of his assistants brought the manifesto from the Century Club across the street. In substance it was this:

"Old Hutch is far from dead. He has had an accident that may prove serious. But not serious enough to permit of any monkey business by certain people in the Wheat Pit. It is announced that all of the wheat sold this morning is now in the hands of Mr. Hutchinson, where it will remain."

Up shot prices again, and the Pit came to attention like a troop of well disciplined soldiers. The Wheat King still lived and still ruled. His word was law. A few hours after his serious injury he had surrounded his bed with a staff of messengers who raced back and forth between him and his brokers. Before the day was over, his bed at the Century Club was a network of telephone wires over which Hutch himself directed the destiny of the world wheat market. He was irrepressible in his determination to see the end of his rainbow. In spite of wracking pain he engineered every detail of the uninterrupted campaign.

Secrecy of deepest hue veiled his injury. One local newspaper commented as follows:

"The Century Club has a peculiar, not so say weird, interest for people in the neighborhood. Some noticed last night that there was a mystery story hanging about the place. Old Hutch was at once made its hero. Not a light was burning in the building located on Pacific Avenue opposite the Board of Trade. Apparently the place was uninhabited. Finally, as this reporter opened a door in a secluded corner of the top floor, a young man who lay half dressed and perspiring on a cot leaped to his feet, as if exposed to an electric battery.

'Where is Mr. Hutchinson's room?'

'Sh—sh—go away quickly!' he wheezed.

'But I want to see Mr. Hutchinson.'

'My friend, you don't know Mr. Hutchinson, or you would not care, or dare, to see him in his present mood.' The reporter left."

It developed that Old Hutch had been found by a servant lying unconscious at the foot of a long flight of iron stairs, when the employee arose at daylight to prepare Mr. Hutchinson's usual early breakfast. Mrs. Hutchinson being in Europe, he had been living at the club. In the middle of the night he had decided to go over once more his compilation of world wheat and bread supplies. In the darkness he opened the wrong door and dived headlong down the flight of slippery iron stairs and lay all night in the open, unconscious, with a broken shoulder and a twisted spine.

After being attended by a physician, who supplied a brace of professional nurses, Old Hutch appointed his own nurses from among his staff of young brokers and then issued one of his characteristic orders:

"Fire those highfalutin nurses. My boys will look after me."

One newspaper made this terse comment on the accident: "Conundrum: If wheat declined three cents, when Old Hutch tumbled down stairs, what should it do if he fell from a balloon?"

A few days elapsed, and then it was announced that the old gentleman's condition was such that he might see visitors. In the next few hours he had received nearly two hundred callers, who included leaders of business, finance, and civic organizations. The first callers, a delegation of bankers, found the old man propped up in bed surrounded by piles of his favorite books. To a group of cronies he was reading from Grey's "Elegy":

> "Let not ambition mock their useful toil,
> Their homely joys, and destiny obscure;
> Nor grandeur hear with a disdainful smile
> The short and simple annals of the poor."

"Well, Mr. Hutchinson," said one of the brokers, "what seems to be your ailment?"

"Iron stairs!" snapped the old man, "And," he added with a twinkle, "it's a hell of a malady. From this day on I am a sworn eternal enemy of iron stairs, and I'm going to see to it that these are replaced within the week.

"I've just been reading to the boys a few choice bits from here and there, and if you gentlemen will be seated you may join in our brief session. Now, for sheer beauty and power listen to this:

> "The moving finger writes; and having writ
> Moves on; nor all your piety nor wit
> Shall lure it back to cancel half a line,
> Nor all your tears wash out a word of it."

"That, boys, is the way of destiny. Do your best, put your whole soul into your undertaking, and let destiny write the result. And, incidentally, it is good policy to follow the suggestion of Napoleon (I believe it was), who said, 'Never complain, and never explain.'

"Verse that is laden with philosophy has helped me all through life. It has been particularly valuable during my campaigns in the Pit. Somehow it opens up the curtains of the mind. I can see and think more clearly. I would be afraid to enter upon an extensive campaign if I were shorn of the mental stimulus obtained from poetry."

Hutchinson's love of verse was as limitless as his ambition to be permanent Wheat King and dictator. In late life, friends who sought his undivided attention would approach him with a bit of verse from one of his favorite authors and then gradually turn to the subject at hand. Any one could reach Old Hutch through the poets.

For three weeks the Wheat King lay on his back analyzing crop reports of all nations, studying supply statistics, directing operations in markets of half a dozen cities, and gorging himself with poetry.

In the face of solemn warnings from physicians, he left his bed and reappeared at the Pit early in August.

His power over the market may be understood when it
is said that his appearance alone brought forth an outburst of cheers from hundreds of adherents, and wheat
prices in the world market shot up two cents.

Then as a further mark of respect and recognition,
the Pit broke precedent and placed on the trading
floor an extremely high wicker chair for the occupancy
of the dictator. It was referred to as "The Throne,"
and there is no evidence indicating that the reference
was distasteful to the Wheat King. There he sat on
his little throne at the north end of the trading hall,
in an angle between the gorgeous limestone pillar and
the public gallery staircase, making and unmaking
markets and, day after day, virtually fixing the precise
figures at which the world might deal in wheat. There
he sat, as immobile as a bronze figure, watching the
hand of the clock registering the price of wheat, unmindful of the hundreds packing the galleries overhead
in the hope of catching a glimpse of him; unmindful,
too, of the deafening noise and clamor, the rumors of
possible wars, the tottering of a throne, or the resigna-
tion of a cabinet. When such reports were thrust upon
him, he only continued watching the clock, or staring
off into space. He knew full well that he would soon
have the market by the throat.

During the entire month of August, Hutchinson was purchasing large quantities of September wheat. Every time the market sagged he would absorb the surplus, and thereafter values would ascend. In the meantime he shipped out enough wheat to create a sound condition. The more he shipped from the central market of the world, the stronger became his power of dictatorship.

Late in the month his campaign was aided by reason of serious frost damage to the growing plant. The more timid "shorts" ran to cover in a panic and paid handsomely for their delinquency.

News of paramount character came to hand late in the month. It took the form of a report from Duluth that there were no receipts of wheat at that point. At about the same time reports from St. Louis showed that May wheat had touched the magic dollar mark, thanks to the subtle generalship of Old Hutch.

Talk of bad conditions in the foreign markets became more prevalent. There was a great deal of surprise and gossip when prices in Europe began soaring. The activity was associated generally with talk of a crop shortage abroad, but there were many who saw the delicate hand of Old Hutch reaching out and touching the right keys on his vast world wheat machine.

Visualizing the immensity of his undertaking a leading Chicago newspaper characterized him as "the greatest speculator ever known. The load he now carries day and night would crush any other operator utterly. But the old man is a giant intellectually, physically, and in will power. A few weeks ago he fell headlong down an iron stairway and lay unconscious with a dislocated spine all night. They doubted if he would ever walk again. Now he is accomplishing alone what no other speculator ever dared to attempt without strong allies at instant command. Where they failed, he has thus far succeeded marvelously. Enraged speculators are already talking wildly about the old man being in danger of assassination. Only yesterday if Hutchinson had insisted upon his pound of flesh a dozen firms would have been crushed before noon."

Big eastern newspapers and magazines began delineating the amazing feats of Old Hutch long before his gigantic deal was completed and long before its breadth and importance were realized. He was commonly called the "Napoleon of Wheat," the greatest speculator of the ages, a wizard of unlimited and uncanny power.

Sensing the importance of what was under way, many special writers were sent out of the East to interview this curious old man of the Pit and to parade his eccentricities before the eyes of the public. All went back empty-handed. One session with Hutch was enough. He never declined to meet the interviewer. But after an exchange of courtesies he would simply refuse to be questioned and with a quick bow turn away with that sturdy inexorable tread of his, setting each foot down as if he meant it to remain there permanently. If pursued, a frown would deepen upon his forehead, his jaw would take on a granite-like set, and his whole bearing would be transformed into bitter belligerency.

Finally he would turn upon the one whom he detested and bellow and hiss with a blasting volley and point the finger of doom with that shivery finality that dammed up the tide of words. In his entire lifetime no one was ever known to have forced a word or an action out of him. He decided his course, and his decisions were as inflexible as his will power. His refusals in business and financial matters of first importance were always arbitrarily final, but touched with a bit of infectious graciousness, his words glinting here and there with genius.

Old Hutch sat upon his miniature throne for only two weeks when he saw the dream of a lifetime gradually taking form and substance. He sat and stared into space and issued an occasional sharp command that kept the markets balanced to a fine delicacy. The mind of a master was accomplishing what had always been, and what has since been, the impossible—a complete corner of the central wheat market.

In September the world rang with the name of Old Hutch.

XI

The Trap Is Sprung

A WHIMSICAL public was proclaiming him the greatest, most picturesque speculator of all ages, the hero of the day. Political reformers were branding him an intolerable tyrant, a gambler in our daily bread. Howling bears and unhappy shorts were dubbing him the "Pirate of the Pit." Old Hutch was unmoved by all the intense feverish excitement. He seemed least concerned of all. Steadily he had climbed upward in Wheat Pit mastery, and now he stood poised on his mountain of opportunity with the aspirations of a lifetime spread out before him.

From opening to closing gong the Pit roared till the rafters shook. Day on day the turmoil grew, until the trading rings became a sea of white up-turned faces, distorted and frantic in expression. The traders were packed in tight and their arms, extended at full length, swung about wildly, tossing up and down like corn stalks in a gale.

The uproar crystalized into a frenzy on August thirty-first, when it became definitely known that Hutch was owner of nearly all the cash wheat in several cities besides Chicago. Confronted with the news, he calmly admitted ownership of most of the physical wheat then in Chicago and made no denial of having extensive outside interests.

"Yes, there is some semblance of truth to these reports," was his laconic comment. "The Pit is always so hungry for news that news just naturally gravitates to the Pit. It has come to pass that my most personal business schemes are flipped about from lip to lip like scandal gossip in a New England village. Life has its crosses."

Still another sensation swept the Pit when Hutch casually admitted that he had chartered a new fleet of lake vessels and intended shipping out of the central market much of the wheat he owned. He said that shipments would be limited only to available vessel space. Up shot wheat, the price in a few days rising from eighty-eight cents to the glorious dollar mark. It was the first time in five years that wheat had sold for a dollar a bushel in Chicago, and reports from the grain belt said that farmers were blessing Old Hutch and that his name was being mentioned at rural prayer meetings.

"Even farmers can say a good word for a speculator, if he happens to be working in their favor," Hutch dryly commented.

On the heels of reports that the old man was carrying his deal to an iron-clad corner, messengers were hurriedly sent to other capitalists at their summer homes and elsewhere. These men were urged to hasten to Chicago for a "finish battle of the Titans," to see whether rulership was permanently to rest with Old Hutch.

"Let them come," he said with a scowl that plainly showed the notion was distasteful. "They can get more action here than in angling for minnows along a muddy river bank."

Just then a clerk stepped up and thrust several letters into his hand.

"Don't bother me," Hutch roared, tearing the letters into bits and flinging them aside without glancing at the contents. "I'm too busy to read mail. Don't you see I'm watching four clocks register grain prices? Anyway, most mail is of no consequence." The clerk hustled away.

In a few days some of the "big boys" did return to the Pit and tried in every possible way to break the impending corner. They heckled Old Hutch and his brokers, offering to negotiate freakish trades that might sway the market from its steady course.

On the morning of September fifth there was a slight uneasiness in the market, and the crowd renewed the heckling tactics under the leadership of Leopold Bloom. Hutchinson brokers tried to ignore the quips and slaps and clownish offers, but the crowd was persistent.

Finally Frank Magin, one of the ablest brokers who ever booted the Wheat Pit with the Hutchinson millions, slipped over to the Throne and whispered his fears to the old man.

"They're making offers we can't with dignity ignore," he complained.

"Now, that's all right, son. Don't you let them bluff you."

"But, chief, suppose they offer to sell me a million bushels in a lump?"

"Take it like a gentleman," retorted the old bull with a toss of his horns.

Magin strolled back into the trading ring. He had no sooner arrived than the robust bulk of Bloom was hovering over him, bellowing new offers.

"Sell you a hundred thousand wheat!" Bloom roared, naming the price.

Magin affected not to hear and started to move away. Bloom blocked his path and, as the bulls and bears listened with amazement, he thundered:

"Sell you a million wheat, with a quarter million dollars up!"

"Sold!" said Hutch's head broker, and he entered the trade on his card.

Bloom shrunk to his normal size instantly and seemed dazed that his boisterous offer had been accepted. He walked slowly away from the trading ring and after a few minutes reappeared on the floor carrying a bundle of green and yellow papers under his arm. Trailed by a crowd of brokers he made his way over to where Hutch sat in his accustomed place by the grand staircase, now as grim and immobile as the sphinx. Bloom proffered the stack of papers.

"Here you are," he said.

"Here I am what?" asked the old man.

"Here are your bonds."

"What bonds? Synagogue bonds?"

"No, railroad bonds; a quarter million dollars' worth, as good as gold."

"Don't want them," said Hutch. "I'm not buying bonds just now. It's wheat I'm after."

"Well, you've got it. I just sold Magin a million bushels for your account, with this quarter million dollars up."

"Well, don't bother me with such inconsequential matters. Go and settle with Magin."

Here Mr. Bloom remembered, by reason of the darkening clouds upon the countenance of the old man, that it annoyed him beyond words to have money or securities flourished in his face. So he went away and found Magin, who accepted the bonds as security for the deal.

"How much did Hutch put up on his side of the deal?" Bloom was asked.

"Of course, Hutch is all right," said Bloom. "He's worth twenty million, and we all know he has never slid out of a deal. His word is his security."

Such was the standing of Old Hutch in the Pit. He could close a million bushel deal with no mention of security.

The single transaction of a million bushels, changing hands in a twinkling with only two individuals involved, was quite extraordinary in those days, or in later days. Usually if a man sold a million or bought a million, the deal was spread among several individuals. So the Hutch-Bloom affair was widely commented upon and had the desired effect for the old plunger. It convinced the Pit that there was extreme danger in making an offer of any magnitude unless the intent was genuine. From that day on, the Hutchinson brokers were subjected to no more confusing distractions.

Shortly after the Bloom bluff was called, several other men of large means began reaching Chicago, while eastern capitalists directed attention to the strange happenings in the Pit. A new alliance of bears was quickly formed for the purpose of dealing one final mighty blow to the sturdy veteran. The stroke came on September nineteenth. The raid of the bears fell like a bolt from the sky. There was no warning. For a time the market wavered under the onslaught; but the sharp crisp orders which Hutch snapped out to his staff of brokers brought the price level back to what the dictator called normal.

Then the unhappy bears found that they had been hopelessly trapped. All the wheat they had sold had again been gathered in by the Hutchinson brokers. When the bears began covering their short sales, prices rushed upward. Now there was nothing for them to do but await development.

This was the last of several bear blows intended to put an end to Old Hutch. After having defeated what the press called "the most powerful bear clique ever formed," he came up smiling with a new offer to buy five million bushels of wheat at a stated price.

On September twentieth Hutch quietly absorbed the last of the offerings, a remarkable feat in light of the fact that no other speculator had ever been able to withstand the eleventh hour downpour of unexpected wheat. Incidentally, a few days later he drew from the clearing house a check for nearly seven hundred thousand dollars, which the press said represented only two days' profits. His iron hand gripped the markets tighter than ever, and he was fast approaching the climax of the historic deal.

Crop reports from the northwest had become worse and worse, and late in the month Minneapolis was asking rates on the shipment of grain from Chicago to the northwest, an unprecedented situation, but one which Hutch had predicted several months previously.

Prices crept up to a dollar twenty-seven on the twenty-seventh day of the month. The Pit was jammed with an excited perspiring mob that fought back and forth across the trading ring during the entire session.

Over by the pillar Old Hutch sat on his little throne, watching the fantastic panorama of a boiling market.

"Do you think this is high?" he asked, when questioned by a group of financiers who were looking over the situation. "The price is quite reasonable to-day. It will be much higher on Saturday. Why, it may even go higher yet to-day," he added, turning to his chief broker with a knowing look. The broker darted for the Pit.

In five minutes new pandemonium reigned, for wheat was climbing by quick sharp leaps. Now it was a dollar ten; now a dollar fifteen; now a dollar eighteen.

"Yes," Old Hutch was saying to the committee, "wheat is worth very much more, but these boys are so contrary they don't seem able to visualize the possibilities. It just doesn't pay to be contrary because——"

From the Pit there rose up above the turmoil a protracted composite groan. All eyes turned upon the price indicator. It registered a dollar twenty-eight!"

"Because," Hutch continued, "an inflexible mind is a dangerous——"

A mob stormed out of the Pit and rushing across the broad floor surrounded the Throne and its occupant. Terror filled the eyes of the puffing, steaming men.

"My God, Mr. Hutchinson, what are you doing to us?" screamed one of them. "You've got us all short, and now you're wringing out our blood!"

"You're wrong, my boy. You've stubbornly made yourselves short, thinking that the big Easterners would undermine and break me and that you would profit by my misery. Now those rascals in the East have not received their punishment yet. It will be far more severe than the spanking you are taking. The game has just only begun."

Off to one side stood a youngish chap, utterly exhausted, his spirit broken. He was brushing tears from his eyes with his coat sleeve. Hutch called him over.

"How much are you out, son?" The young man whispered an amount. Hutch made a notation on a card and handed it to him with instructions to see his chief clerk, and the chap hustled away smiling.

"Have to look out for young fellows. It's the old ducks that don't need sympathy."

Once more Hutch surveyed the crowd before him. They had turned from feverish excitement to quiet dejection. They waited for some word of hope from the dictator.

"I'm going to give you fellows one more chance to be good. Here Johnny," he called to John Brine, one of his assistants. "Let these boys have what wheat they want for the next ten minutes at a dollar and a quarter a bushel. But remember, not one bushel for an eastern account."

The crowd quickly formed in two lines straggling off from the pillar, at the base of which sat the architect of their fate, flanked by two aides who wrote on cards at his dictation, as he agreed with one after another to settle at a dollar and a quarter.

It was the wildest day in months. Margin clerks worked far into the night.

"Do you anticipate any failures along the street?" Hutch was asked.

"No. I have seen to that."

Late in the day there were rumors that special trains loaded with wheat were being brought in from St. Louis and Milwaukee in a new attempt to break the impending corner.

"Let it come," was his comment. "I'll take all they want to offer at a dollar and a half."

Next day the press reported that Hutch could have

dictated a much higher price and forced the shorts to cover. "So completely was the market in his power that several hundred thousand bushels which he sold during the day at a dollar and a quarter were delivered back to him at eighty-five cents. . . . His gains for the day were enormous."

Shortly after daylight Hutch was on the job. When a pale emaciated looking elevator boy complained to his companion that he had no overcoat, the old man took off his own new coat and handed it to the lad without comment.

After spending an hour or two reviewing crop reports and studying the news of the morning, he drifted over to his little throne and settled down for a "right smart day." It annoyed him somewhat to observe that the galleries were packed with spectators, who hoped for a glimpse of the new Wheat King. Most of them had brought their lunches and planned to spend the day. For a few minutes he looked sour and appeared restless under the gaze of the curious. Then he pulled his slouch hat deep over his face and turned up his collar, completely shielding his features from the stare of the crowd.

With a roar that reverberated up and down La Salle street the market swung underway at the booming of the gong. In thirty minutes Old Hutch had driven the price up ten cents. He sat by his pillar, grim and relentless, keeping his eyes upon the wheat indicator and now and then issuing new orders to his little army of brokers. In another half hour the price had jumped ten cents more.

A half-crazed plunger rushed up to the old man.

"I'll give you one forty for wheat!" he fairly shouted. "That's the last price made in the Pit."

"Calm yourself," said Hutch in a low voice. "I've decided to make the price of wheat a dollar and a half."

And to the consternation of the grain world he fixed the price at one fifty, and two minutes later wheat was quoted at that level in the central world market. No longer could there be any doubt of his power. Every one recognized that the greatest corner in wheat history was now an indisputable fact.

As the trading day drew to a close, the market quieted down. The King climbed from his throne and began walking slowly about the floor with a few of his friends. In a jiffy the pits were empty and a long line of brokers was trailing after the ruler, listening for each word, and hoping against hope for some ray of light. Old Hutch talked of Tom Paine and Liberty, of the French Revolution, of the mistakes of Napoleon.

He poured out a rich fund of historical knowledge with hardly a pause. But on the subject so near the hearts of his auditors he said not a word. As he departed for his club some one made so bold as to ask the probable course of wheat, to which he replied:

"To-morrow will be a tolerably busy day."

XII

Step Up to the Captain

LONG before dawn Old Hutch awakened to the most momentous day of his intense life. It had not been a sleepless night with horrible misshapen phantoms sweeping through the chambers of the brain. He said later it had been one of those dreamless nights that make the sleeper almost enamoured of death. He awakened refreshed and of good spirit. White fingers of light gradually crept through the curtains, and the black shadows crawled off into the corners. He watched veil after veil of thin dusky gauze being lifted; he saw the dawn remake the world into its old familiar patterns.

As he lay there thinking of the ambitions of his youth, all the dreams of a lifetime flooded his mind, soothing him, lulling him into a sense of peace. Now he felt that at last his one great aim was being accomplished. The hour of victory had arrived. Here indeed was a day worth living.

He arose, ate a hearty breakfast, and was seated in the exchange hall long before the vanguard of early risers began putting in an appearance. His attention was riveted upon a small pad of paper containing columns of figures he had compiled, representing the wheat supplies at each of the domestic markets and at all the pivotal points in Europe.

While he was thus engrossed, a messenger stepped up beside him.

"Mr. Hutchinson, your son would like to see you at once. It is most important. He is in his office."

The old man immediately set off, mumbling over this distraction but confident too that the call must concern matters of utmost consequence. Charlie had never before summoned him in this hasty fashion.

He did not pause at the threshold of his son's office, but stepped briskly inside, closing the door behind him. A moment later there was a clicking sound as the bolt of the lock slipped home. Exactly what transpired behind locked doors in the next thirty minutes between the great speculator and his youthful son, one of the ablest business men in the city's history, was never revealed. But it may be well imagined, from subsequent events, that the conversation was along some such line as this:

"Father, something drastic must be done and done at once. Your immense deal in wheat has reached a magnitude far beyond anything that had been suspected. The street is in a turmoil. The speculative markets are boiling over. The whole country is in an uproar over what is taking place. Large depositors are threatening to boycott our bank. Mutterings are being heard over the price of bread. Labor groups are crying out against you. There have even been whispered warnings that your life is in danger.

"Surely you are not blinded to the seriousness of the situation. It is true that you have violated no law; nor have you broken any rule of the exchanges, for unfortunately the exchanges now have no anti-corner rule, though they should have, and they will have.

"My appeal to you is grounded on something more sacred; something that strikes deeper than laws and rules and regulations. I have in mind your pledge."

The old man must have gone pale at the thought.

"You will recall that when you urged me to accept the presidency of the exchange you pledged your word to abide by my wishes under all conditions and in the face of all circumstances."

"But, son, don't you realize that I have given a lifetime of study and planning to this effort?"

"I am sorry, father. I cannot know the workings of your mind. Perhaps you have the power to go on cornering the next wheat future, and the next, and the next, until finally you wield a mighty power over traffic in grain. Personally, I doubt it; but we have no concern now with that point. We both know your pledge. And on that pledge I must now exercise my right and urge you to release your grip, to sell sufficient wheat to relieve this terrible crisis."

That was enough. Charles Hutchinson knew his father. He knew that the old warrior would rather give his life than break his word. And last of all would he break his word to his son, for between them there had always existed a strong bond of love. Charles Hutchinson must have known too the pain his father felt when the house of cards began tumbling over his head. It was indeed a stirring moment for the old dreamer. What a feeling of despair must have engulfed him when once more he saw his hopes dashed to earth and shattered to bits.

But already he had made up his mind. He would fulfill his obligation to his son. But by no means would he let his enemies, the big bears, go scot free. They would pay and pay dearly.

Slowly but with steady tread he made his way back to the trading floor, which was now coming to life. As he strode directly toward the little throne, he seemed not to hear the shouting of messengers, the clatter of telegraph keys, the outcries of traders starting for the rings, the whirring telephones, and the shuffle and scrape of a thousand feet, all of which mingled in a high pitched rumble, sustained and unbroken, that echoed through the airy roof and issued from every opening of the building. As the minute approached for the market to swing under way, the staccato clicking of the wire instruments rose to a din. The throaty hum of the murmuring crowd swelled like a rising tide.

He had hardly reached his chair when suddenly, slashing through the dim rumble of the floor came the sharp incisive boom of the gong starting the day's trading. In a flash all the noise and disorder of a bedlam were unchained. Words and phrases were lost in the jumbled thunder of sound. Brokers snatched at each other, bellowed offers for wheat, stumbled, stamped about, and with arms stretched high signaled the prices —ever rising prices—which they would pay for the coveted yellow grain.

The eyes of Hutch were fastened upon the great dial,

a dial with a hand that indicated the price of wheat. With the first outburst of trading the hand trembled slightly, and then began moving upward on its course. Long since it had passed the one fifty mark, and traders were thrown into a worse panic than had hitherto swept the worn floors of the Pit.

Hutch knew he must do something. He must keep his pledge. He had a new responsibility. He must save the market, prevent a streak of failures on the street, and still mete out the punishment he felt his enemies deserved. And, incidentally, pile up new millions.

He called his chief broker.

"Let them have some wheat," he said in a low, cold voice.

"Why, sir, you're not——?"

"Let them have some wheat!"

The broker rushed back to the Pit and began selling to the hungry bears, who tumbled over each other in an effort to cover.

"Sell some more!" ordered Old Hutch when a lull came.

More wheat was sold, then more. But when it looked as if Hutch might be deliberately breaking his own corner, a sharp order from him stopped further sales.

He had kept his promise. He had lightened his grip. He had turned loose some of his holdings, about seven million bushels of cash wheat and futures, "enough to prevent a riot," as he phrased it; but he still remained dictator of the market.

With a tinge of bitterness toward fate, Hutch himself admitted that his son had called the halt, disclaiming any moderation on his own part.

"Mind you, I didn't tell Charlie what I would do," he said. "But I made up my mind to follow his wishes. I neither deserve nor desire any credit for leniency. It was all Charlie. I never really knew him until to-day. He is worth his weight in gold." Perhaps love and pride in his son proved more of a solace than ambition, for Hutch repeated over and over again, "I never knew him until to-day."

The market thundered on and on after the brief lull incident to the flair of compassion on the part of the dictator. The hand of the indicator continued trembling between quotations but its course was steadily forward.

Of a sudden a new edict came from the throne. It was terse and startling. It caused rage and despair among the big bears; for most of those leaders had not covered during the momentary selling by which Old

Hutch had kept his pledge. They did not cover because Hutch deftly saw to it that they were ignored. Now came this new order from the King to add to their maddening predicament:

"I have decided wheat is worth two dollars a bushel!"

"Has Old Hutch gone stark mad? In these enlightened times can he enforce such arbitrary price-making upon the central grain market of the entire world? Is there no power to stop him? Why, only a week ago wheat was selling at a dollar a bushel; and that magic price was the highest figure in five years." Thus the gossip swept across the trading floor amid the overhead tumult of the market. The quick price gyrations that came on the heels of the edict were confirmation enough of his determination and of his power. The corner was beyond doubt a genuine success, made so by the bold and daring use of millions by a genius of remarkable capabilities.

Foolish little dramas have a way of creeping into big scenes where they do not belong. The Wheat Pit, most sensitive of all the delicate indicators of price trend, responds in a flash to the unusual. Now there was a new commotion which suddenly stilled the wheels of the marketing machinery during the biggest and most dramatic corner in history. The roar had suddenly ceased. The Pits became quiet. All eyes were turned toward the main entrance to the floor, through which a maddened broker was wedging his way between crowds and advancing toward the trading rings, bellowing:

"I am shot! I am shot!"

Spectators in the packed galleries rushed for rail positions to look down upon the lunatic. Hutch sat calmly on his throne, firm and unsmiling, and watched the drama with apparent indifference.

A dozen traders seized the distraught and screaming broker to examine his wounds. After a time he was quieted.

"Who did it?" some one asked.

"Old Hutch," the man replied in tones of agony.

The report that Hutch had shot a man spread like lightning. The crowd was in just the right temper to believe anything of the old gentleman.

"Where are you shot?" the man was asked.

He stared stupidly for a moment.

"I didn't say 'shot.' I said 'short,' " he replied. "Old Hutch did it."

A groan went up from the crowd. Whereupon the unhappy short was led to the side of Old Hutch, who healed his wounds by letting him cover his wheat at a low price. Then the man was taken off to see his physician, and the roar of the Pit was renewed.

In another hour all the fight had at last gone out of the big bears, as well as out of the brokers who represented large Eastern capital. Gradually the market had tightened up so that very little wheat was changing hands. The end was in sight. In a period of two weeks Hutch had pushed up the price of wheat, a world commodity, from ninety cents to two dollars a bushel, where it now stood, and had climaxed his amazing feat by raising the price twenty-five per cent over night.

He had said he would do it, and he did it, amid a turmoil that echoed from coast to coast, amid the bitter outbursts from the labor leaders, who accused him of robbing the poor by putting up the price of bread. While his ears rang with the fiery protests of a thousand separate groups, he sat upon his little throne and with no change of facial expression, without so much as the flicker of an eyelash, looked out over the mob of angry bears spread across the floor in front of him and thundered: "Boys, step up to the captain!"

The game was up for the bears. They were trapped, with no hope of escape. There remained but one recourse, and that was to "step up to the captain," which meant to turn their contracts in to Old Hutch, and thereupon make settlement with that solemn gentleman on his own terms. Those terms were now two dollars a bushel for wheat.

One by one the badly battered bears held conclave with the dictator, who was determined and unbending when dealing with those of large means. It happened now and then that the vanquished rival would give vent to his feelings, unbridling his tongue to comment that cut deeply into the old man despite his apparent lack of interest. He would listen with patience. At the end he was always ready to meet the thrust. His teeming brain took in raw suggestions and molded them into polished phrases, epigrams and symbols which were tossed out in a manner most disarming. Usually he was able to turn the wrath of the antagonist into good humored fun, especially if there were onlookers present to catch up his slow, dry wit with its curious infectiousness.

With the most unruly bears he parried and countered as long as argument seemed useful. Then he became vividly dynamic; his vitality sparkled and glittered; his anger rose to fire and fury. His tongue would lash out in a withering tirade. And the noisy bear would become meekly silent. Hutch was king.

To the unfortunate weaklings who were stupid enough to get caught in the trap and to the heads of firms that had inadvertently been drawn in, Hutch would whisper these consoling words which over a long period of years so endeared him to the Street:

"Put your differences in the clearing house, and we'll settle quietly between ourselves later on."

The great corner was thus concluded without a failure on the street.

"Those who are worst bitten," said a leading newspaper, editorially, "cannot accuse Hutch of malice or want of interest in the welfare of the market. They all know full well that had he called margins on the advances, houses would have collapsed by the dozen before a dollar fifty had been reached. Custom would have sanctioned such a course. Every other corner in the history of speculation had provided a precedent. But the old man was magnanimous."

The feverish day, a day of torture for the enemies of Hutch, finally drew to a close. Little remained of the immense corner except the work of clearing up the debris, settling the accounts of rebellious shorts who had point blank refused to "step up to the captain." But such holdouts were of no great consequence and eventually they settled just as Hutch had said they would settle "after their spunk subsides, and they quit pouting."

After the close of the market Hutch had held open house to the recalcitrants from the little throne. This work continued until a fixed hour late that day, and then he was through with business. All efforts to draw him into talk of wheat were futile.

"Have you heard of my latest purchase?" he asked the group. "Well, I have bought an old history of the Hutchinson who was governor of the colony of Massachusetts during the revolution. It's quite valuable. I think my next purchase will be an exceptionally fine edition of Ruskin's works. I've had my eye on it. Now some of those English authors are splendid."

"Mr. Hutchinson, if I paid you two dollars for wheat——"

The interruption was ignored.

"It will be a long time before we have men like them over here. We have no Shakespeares or Bacons, no Sir Walter Scotts or Sir Joshua Reynolds."

"Let me ask you about wheat, Mr. Hutchinson."

"Now, I'll tell you. Talmage is the greatest man we have had since Beecher died."

Thus the Wheat King topped off a memorable day, chatting of literature, of art, music, philosophy; of wars and revolutions; of religion and politics. But not one word of wheat. He was weary of the subject.

Slowly the floor emptied. The tide had turned to the big open doorways. Spectators who had watched the drama of the Pit from the galleries had been reluctant to leave. They had wanted the show to go on. But now the galleries were cleared, and the immense floor was empty except for an occasional straggler. The pits and trading floor, swept clean as a ship deck in the morning, were littered with grain, crumpled message blanks, orange parings, torn newspapers, and thousands of memoranda wrinkled and soiled from the trampling of an army of feet.

Old Hutch sat alone on his little throne looking out over the battle field strewn with the scraps of war. He was weary and downcast. But he was not thinking of what might have been. Like the true speculator he was looking ahead. His corner was at an end. He had made millions, but his immediate complete mastery had ended with the close of the deal in September wheat. He had wanted power, continuing power, far more than he wanted millions. Money was only the key that unlocked the door to power. Otherwise it was of no consideration. Of course there would be new opportunities. Next year might prove even more propitious for gain-ing permanent mastery. It probably would. And besides he would have no binding pledges to fulfill. He would be free. And now he could wait. No hurry; the market would always be there.

Thus he mused while the troup of night shift cleaners, spread out fan-shaped, began guiding broad brooms across the spacious hall, and batteries of steaming tanks were rolled in by the mop crew.

Then the Wheat King departed.

XIII

On Trial

THE brilliant star of Old Hutch was glittering in the speculative skies. His name was on every lip. The press of the world raked the dumps of speculative history in quest of parallel deeds of daring. Special meetings were called by this group and that. Some sought to blacken his name; others to laud his genius. His act had at least proved a boon to farmers. Wheat prices were sky high.

He went stolidly about the work of clearing up innumerable complications of the big deal. He made short shift of the "committee of debtors" formed by Eastern interests to prevail upon him for leniency with the hold-outs, those who had refused to settle.

"Why are you annoying me with your silly offers?" he stormed. "My price for wheat is two dollars."

William Young stepped forward and closed his account at that figure. It was a break in the ranks, and soon others followed until finally the whole score was cleared.

Then Old Hutch slept, not for a few hours, but for the best part of three days. He threw his tired body upon a couch in his private room at the Corn Exchange bank and remained there until his immense vitality returned and roused him to action.

"What is the press saying?" That was the question uppermost in his mind upon recuperating from the long drain on his strength. It was the first time he had indicated the slightest interest in public opinion.

Some of the headlines of the past few days were read to him. They were harsh, humorous, and laudatory: "Old Hutch is a monster. . . . He is a sordid, soulless speculator. . . . The silent unmurmuring millions will seal his fate. . . . Old Hutch is a hero. . . . The big Easterners had sought to pick his bones. . . . A triumph for Yankeedom. . . . Massachusetts should erect a statue to him. . . . Another cent is added to bread. . . . Size of five cent loaf shrinks. . . . Mothers quiet babies with name of Old Hutch. . . . Profits of Hutch are eight million dollars. . . . It's nip and tuck between Old Nick and Old Hutch."

Paragraphers poked fun at the battered bears. With

their rollicking quips and bits of verse they did a great deal toward swaying public opinion to the side of the veteran plunger.

"Old Hutch a silken robe de nuit
Can wear on his lordly back
The rascals whom he roped in wheat
Can sleep in a gunny sack."

In a period of two weeks the bitterness had in large measure subsided. That fickle jade, public opinion, was again doing an about-face. Most every one wanted to say a good word for the picturesque adventurer. Theaters rang with his name, and even in the pulpits kindly mention was made of his genius, and the hope expressed that his powers might now be turned to deeds of greater good.

Friends sought to visit him, but he would talk to no one. He spent little time at the Pit. He did not have to. The yawning throne was sufficient to terrorize the bears and keep things in order. A report that he was in a New York hotel drew a curious milling throng, which the police were forced to disperse. Notables passing through Chicago asked in vain for interviews. One young chap, a comedian, persisted so strongly in his request for a chat with the Wheat King that the old man finally gave in on the one condition that he would be made to laugh. The interview lasted two hours, ending only when the comedian was forced to catch his train, and only after he had forced the sullen old plunger to roar until his sides ached. The young comedian who had lifted Hutch out of the doldrums into high good humor was Nat Goodwin. Later the two became close friends.

Gossip in and out of the Pit now turned to the probable future plans of the Wheat King. He was genuinely feared by the big leaders, bulls and bears alike, not only in Chicago but in the other markets. At the same time he had endeared himself to the rank and file of brokers and traders, and his support was national in scope. By virtue of his amazing corner he had attained the impossible, and his power had been magnified to immense proportions in the minds of traders. Therefore he was given a wide berth. His word was law.

It has been forty years since the running of the historic corner. And in all that time there has been recurring conjecture as to what end Hutch might have attained, if he had not been held in bounds by an entangling pledge; if he had carried out his original plan of gradually extending the corner.

Some speculative critics have contended that to extend his power to other markets and to gain permanent price mastery would have been an utter impossibility. They believe that fundamental conditions were all favorable to Hutch and that his exceptional genius made it possible for him to visualize coming events and, like an able general, to marshall all his forces into carefully chosen strategic positions. After which he had but to signal for the closing of the giant pincers upon the wheat market. Without favorable conditions, such as the crop disaster in one important section, he never could have engineered so great a corner. So much for the doubtful ones.

Opposite views are taken by other critics. They point out that not only was the marketing machinery clumsy and imperfect in those days, lending itself to such plans as churned about in the brain of Old Hutch, but that the crop was smaller and less difficult to encompass. They admit that Hutch needed every advantage in his favor, and they say that the release of even a small part of his holdings put an end temporarily to thought of establishing a permanent dictatorship over wheat prices. But as one student of markets has pointed out, if there is the slightest merit in the proposal for an export wheat corporation, backed by the government, to take the American surplus off the market for the purpose of maintaining high domestic prices—a proposal that has disturbed congress in recent years—then the dream of Old Hutch was not beyond the border of possibility. By a series of gigantic corners in wheat he had visions of controlling the surplus and of also controlling enough of the needed supply to dictate prices. If such control could be effected by government subsidy, why could it not have been obtained by the powerful master of speculation, operating directly through the marketing machinery? Students of marketing say the weakness rests in the fact that if any attempt were made to keep prices higher than justified by economic law, wheat growing would prove so attractive that the volume of production would swell beyond all limits of consumption. Then the scheme would fall of its own weight. Perhaps Old Hutch knew this and realized that the power to dictate high prices, even if it were definitely acquired, could not be extended beyond a period of a few years, or until overproduction developed. Or perhaps he had some scheme for harmonizing high prices and excessive production, which, however, is improbable.

But he never explained any of his plans concerning wheat market operations, not even to his most intimate associates. So his grand dreams still remain a perpetual riddle to the Pit.

After the close of the September corner, Hutch did not swing heavily into the next wheat future, which was December wheat, with a view to repeating the coup sixty days hence. He only toyed with the market in a manner designed to keep it at a strong level and to lay the ground work for his campaign the following year. Despite his disappointment he still solemnly believed that he was the fated master of the Wheat Pit and all that it meant to commerce. Again he must prepare for the day. He must watch and wait.

Meantime he had many personal matters of importance that deserved attention; at least they seemed important to Old Hutch. There was, for instance, the suit against him for twenty-eight dollars. He would fight that to the bitter end. He would see if justice still reigned in the courts.

For many months the Century Club, where Hutch was director general, and sometimes chef, had been the object of much gossip. Those who for one reason or another were denied the privilege of entering its stately portals were prone to spread whispered tales about its gayety and the magnitude of its jack-pots. A rigid club rule laid down by Hutch prohibited members from babbling of club affairs outside the club, and this rule was strictly adhered to save for the occasional whimpering of some crony who complained of the food and believed himself a martyr to the culinary ambitions of the old plunger.

But it was obvious that the whispered stories discrediting the club were sheer fables fashioned to embarrass the director general. Finally, through the suspected connivance of his enemies, the affairs of the Century Club exploded in open court.

Mrs. Thirze Manning was the complainant. She was suing H. C. Cardwell for a twenty-eight dollar loan. Hearing that Cardwell at one time "mixed drinks and kept tab" at the club, and that money might be owing him for such service, the father of the club was dragged into court, his affidavit that he never employed Cardwell being rejected. It looked like a crudely trumped up scheme to publicly flay Old Hutch and his exclusive little club.

Hutch was in a rare temper when he climbed the stairs to the court of Justice Jarvis Bloom. He was in a rage after having waited in vain all afternoon for the judge to show up. Messages came from his Honor from time to time saying he was downtown but would be along in good season. At nightfall the case was postponed to the following day.

The stuffy little court room was crowded next afternoon, when the head of the Century Club, with his great black hat pulled low over the eyes, and his granite chin set forward in a belligerent challenge, stepped briskly through the doorway and inquired if the judge had finally arrived.

Charles A. Orvis was the first witness examined. He swore that Cardwell never had been employed by Old Hutch or by the club, but had sought shelter for a time and was given odd jobs by some of the members, whose gratuities were later pooled and handed to the ne'er-do-well with advice to be on his way.

That testimony was not enough. The scalp of Old Hutch was sought. He was ordered to the stand, and at once climbed into the swaying swivel chair that topped a crude platform.

Attorney Clark, counsel for the defense, was a giant of a fellow with great limbs and heavy shoulders. As he stood across the table glaring at the Plunger and bellowing his questions, his bulk, his fierce black whiskers, and his thundering voice were intended to inspire terror.

"Now, what is your business, Mr. Hutchinson?"

"Commission merchant."

"Was Cardwell ever in your employ?"

"No."

"Now, what do you mean?" The lawyer shouted.

"Just what I say, you chump! Do you call me a liar?"

There was commotion as bailiffs pushed back the crowd.

"I want answers to my questions. Was Cardwell at work about the Century Club?"

"Yes, for a week."

"O-ho, he was, was he?"

"Are you deaf? You heard my answer."

"Now, what is your connection with the club, Mr. Hutchinson?"

"Haven't any."

"You mean you're not a member?"

Before the court could rule out the question as irrelevant, Hutch had unrolled a formidable parchment piped with gold and red seals and tied with varicolored ribbons. It was the club charter. Then he submitted a book containing a roll of members. To the surprise of all his name was not included.

The lawyer continued blazing away with sarcastic

questions reflecting upon the character of the club.

"Is the club anything more than a poker and drinking den?" he shouted.

"None of your damned business!" stormed the witness.

"Stop, at once," Judge Bloom broke in. "You must know, Mr. Hutchinson, that I cannot permit such language in this court room."

"Now, Mr. Hutchinson," the lawyer continued, "what does this book amount to? Couldn't any tramp or bum with a membership fee join your club?"

"We would bar a pettifogger like you," was the retort.

The lawyer pressed on. "Hasn't this club a demoralizing influence?"

"It would make a Christian of the likes of you," Hutch replied amid an outburst of laughter.

Again the court warned counsel and witness that they would be fined for contempt if the tirade continued. "Take your books and papers, Mr. Hutchinson. They cannot be used as evidence," said the court.

Hutch reached for them, whereupon the big attorney planked both hands down upon them. For a moment the old man glared over his long nose at his burly tormenter. Then he took a quick step forward and with a wide vicious right-hand swing cut the air with his fist, just as Judge Bloom leaned over and, seizing the lawyer's shoulders, yanked him out of range of the onrushing fist.

"Gentlemen, gentlemen, this must stop!" puffed Judge Bloom, his face florid from the exertion. "It is disgraceful. I shall end the case right here. Mr. Hutchinson is discharged. There is no evidence against him. Court is adjourned." All happened in a jiffy.

Old Hutch slowly folded up the imposing charter of the Century Club, gathered his books in his arm, and walked leisurely to the door. Then turning sharply about he waved his fist at the bustling attorney and shouted:

"You insulting, pettifogging scamp! I urgently invite you to step to the street level and question me."

The big trial of the famous Century Club, which had been anticipated with glee by the gossip mongers and the enemies of the Wheat King, was at an end. Instead of being a bomb, it had been a complete fizzle.

Later in the afternoon Hutch returned to court and apologized to Judge Bloom, who graciously excused his conduct and placed full blame upon the attorney.

Then the Wheat King invited court attaches, witnesses, and spectators to a party at a nearby café where he addressed them on the subject of whiskers.

"You know," he said, "I might have gotten on better if that fellow hadn't kept thrusting his whiskers at me. I have always detested whiskers. A man should step out in the open. His face should be revealed, so that his heart may be read. Whiskers conceal too many things. More than one humbug has taken refuge behind an insanitary hedge."

XIV

Washed in the Blood

WHEN Old Hutch next appeared at the Pit and mounted his little throne, a murmur of surprise rippled across the spacious hall. Traders tried to appear unconcerned as they stole quick, fleeting glances at the Wheat King. Messenger boys hid their smiles and muffled their twitterings. The stern face and glowering eyes of the ruler stemmed the tide of any clownish buffoonery that might have been aimed at his new regalia.

The object of the surprise and suppressed merriment was the crown worn by the King. He had discarded his famous old black hat with its broad floppy brim. In its place he wore an amazingly high silk tile, a hat that added nearly a foot and a half to his own unusual height. Hutch was King, and he had crowned himself. The "Napoleon of Wheat" had not emulated the great Bonaparte by seizing the crown from a Pope at the crucial moment and clapping it on with his own hands.

The occasion had been without pomp or ceremony. He had simply selected the silk tile at the most exclusive shop in town and jammed it down firmly against the ears, where it remained.

On the same day he had broken still another precedent. He had stopped at the tobacco stand of the exchange and stuffed his pockets with ten cent cigars, which later were passed out to the chosen few. Nickel cigars had always served quite well before. But now Old Hutch was doing a bit of celebrating over the profits of his big deal, profits variously estimated at from three to eight millions of dollars, the exact figure never being definitely known.

For the next few weeks the silk tile added a tone of dignity and splendor to the market, as Hutch plowed in and out, lashing the Pit to his will, and whipping prices up and down as judgment or fancy might dictate.

"The future biographer of the Wheat King," commented the editor of a leading daily, "will be apt to devote a great deal of space to the remarkable ease with which he leaps from one side of the market to the other in the game which Joaquin Miller declared Napoleon, if he were alive, would find a more fitting field for his talents than war.

"No other giant speculator can shift so quickly. Monday he crushed the life out of the market with the weight of millions of bushels of wheat that he sold. He was the boldest of bears. Yesterday he was a rampant bull. He bought back all he had sold and a great deal more. His power was seldom better illustrated."

In his flashing raids in and out of the market, Hutch took great pains to punish his enemies. He would batter away at them deliberately, complacently, sometimes announcing his intentions in advance, after the unruly ones had ventured upon dangerous grounds. In a single day he lambasted R. G. Tenant marketwise, and then, in the presence of the whole Pit, verbally denounced him and excommunicated him from further trading with Hutchinson brokers; he poured out a torrent of accusations against Walter Chapman; and J. C. Gowell and Finley Brown were figuratively stood on their heads. "Too many rowdies," the old man grumbled.

Then there was the oily Mr. Bloom, who seemed always to nettle the ruler of the Pit. It was decreed at length that Bloom should be given a major licking instead of a mere spanking. The press reported the episode tersely: "Bloom made himself very offensive to the old man, who now takes sweet revenge, for Bloom leaves a big bundle of securities behind. It will be many a day before the wily Bloom seeks introduction to another buzz saw."

Many tales are told concerning the multiplying eccentricities of Old Hutch during the period following his famous corner. Large deeds, some of them magnanimous to the last degree, were intermingled with bitter quarrels over trifles. He would haggle and chaffer over the price of some simple article and at the same time pass out large loans to the deserving in the absence of any security.

He reveled in his ability to strike a sharp bargain. When a fruit store near the exchange insisted upon charging three cents for apples, he started his own store next door and sold apples at a cent apiece, until the rival merchant came to terms. He thought fifteen cents was too much for the boys to pay for whiskey, so he began a warfare that pulled the price down to two drinks for a quarter.

Scrubwomen at the exchange were paid little enough in those days. So, in moments of good humor, Hutch would have them dance and sing for the crowd in the evening, giving each a silver dollar as reward. Their harsh voices, raised in a polyglot discord, and their clumsy steps to the tune of improvised music brought gales of laughter. They called Hutch the "good boss" and in hours of trouble knew that his chief clerk would advance a week's wages.

He was not by nature a social creature, but when time permitted the mood, he fraternized with all, high and low. There is the story of the "dago dinner." For a few days it was the talk of the town. As one newspaper reported it: "Mrs. Hutchinson had issued invitations to a group of ladies for a five o'clock tea. Under her orders the table had been prepared in advance of the hour set for the arrival of the guests. On that particular afternoon Mr. Hutchinson came home earlier than usual. His wife was engaged in making her toilet. There was a meal for a dozen or twenty, and Old Hutch saw no one about to eat it. He remembered a gang of men on the street nearby digging a sewer and recalled that they appeared tired and hungry. The next minute he had invited them in, bade them welcome, and seated them at the table over which he presided. By the time Mrs. Hutchinson returned to that part of the house all were gone. And so was the 'tea'."

Reports had it that Hutch gave the rugged sons of

Italy one of his vivid talks on patriotism, and elicited a pledge from each that he would strive to be a good, loyal American and, moreover, that he would refrain from the use of garlic in his chosen land.

Most any derelict could touch the heart strings of Hutch in his later years. Many hopeless fellows, burned down to the stub end of soiled lives, were helped into cleaner surroundings and given a new lease on life. But he was no dupe and insisted that every honest man must work. Being approached one day by a strapping big tramp, Hutch said:

"Do you see that stone there? Well, you carry it to the next corner and back. Rest one minute between trips. I'll pay you five dollars a day until a better job can be found."

The tramp made two trips and quit cold.

"There," said Hutch, "goes the symbol of social stagnation and mental decay."

In the wake of the big wheat deal came a number of suicides in various parts of the country. Some of them were attributed to worry over market losses. The Toledo Produce Exchange called attention to "the list of suicides among the unlucky speculators." When Col. Charles T. Hatch, a prominent railroad man of Minneapolis, shot himself in his office, the *Commercial*

Bulletin called him "another victim of the tragic deal in wheat." As the *New York Herald* pointed out, however, the suicides had no connection with the Hutchinson deal. "From all accounts it would seem as if Old Hutch were a sort of two-legged Juggernaut, who helped the coroner and his deputies long after office hours. Almost every case of suicide or insanity within two hundred miles of Chicago during the last few months has been laid to financial worry over losses in the wheat corner."

By no stretch of the imagination could any of the suicides be traced directly to the big deal, and after this became indisputably apparent, Hutch was completely vindicated by the press. But the thought that such a cloud should hang over him for even a day was extremely painful to one of his sensitive nature. He must have brooded long and hard over the unjust reflection and over the finely veiled innuendoes flipped about by his rivals. One of his rules of life had been to do his fellow man no wrong. In spite of his iron handed rulership, his grandiose schemes for power, and his vicious lashes at the markets, Old Hutch was indeed imbued with a high sense of honesty and solemnly believed himself fair and honorable in all dealings, both business and personal. The many contradictions in his nature appearing in late years, and the paradoxical whims that seemed so grotesque in light of his straight and sturdy mental course earlier in life, sometimes threw his acts open to adverse comment. But no one ever questioned his fundamental goodness or his sense of honor. Those whom he deliberately injured were men who chose to cross swords with him in the battle for power.

Long after the suicides episode had been forgotten, Hutch would deftly bring up the subject in talks with his cronies, as if seeking to confirm his hope that not the slightest blame could possibly rest upon him. The distasteful memory clung to him like an ugly, misshapen dream. He knew he had been responsible for no suicides; yet the ghastly thought that some people might think otherwise seemed to fasten itself upon his mind and claw at his quickening nerves.

How long the disturbing thoughts remained is not known. Nor is there any evidence that they ever had the slightest influence upon the future life of the Wheat King. It is interesting to note, however, that, outwardly at least, he gave more thought to the spiritual side of life.

After one particularly strenuous day, Hutch sat long in his stuffy little office meditating over the past and dreaming of the future. At last he closed his desk and walked out into the street.

The starlit night, glittering and somber, seemed to hang like a splendid drapery. The air was crisp and exhilarating, and Old Hutch, always a vigorous walker when seeking exercise, stepped along at a lively clip. After half an hour his pace slackened in front of a little church. The door stood ajar in welcome. From within he could hear the booming hallelujahs of the faithful. Perhaps from sheer curiosity, or for the purpose of resting a few moments, he stepped inside and dropped into a rear seat.

Sermons in those days were still powerfully searching, even to the dividing asunder of the joints and marrow. No less vigorous were some of the hymns telling of the torture of after life for the tardy sinner who failed to see the light. It was one such hymn that had startled old Daniel Drew, pioneer Wall Street speculator, into "accepting the Lord," after some of his early business sins had seared deeply into his soul. The precise hymn that set old Uncle Dan to building churches and seminaries bearing his name had plenty of life and get up:

"Waken and mourn, ye heirs of hell,
Let stubborn sinners fear;
You must be driven from earth, to dwell
A long Forever there.

See how the pit gapes wide for you,
And flashes in your face.
And thou, my soul, look downwards too,
And sing recovering grace!"

Perhaps it was some such hymn that seized the imagination of the rapidly aging Hutch, and made him feel the religious surge beat in his veins. Perhaps he was merely amused and enjoyed the atmosphere of religious fervor. At any rate, as explained by the *Inter-Ocean*, he became a regular attendant at various churches; "And the harder the preacher pitched into the wicked, and the more he said about a literal hell, the better Mr. Hutchinson liked it. His tall, angular form could be seen nearly every night in the Amen Corner of some church, where the services promised to be particularly lively. No one rolled out the hymns and the hallelujahs like Old Hutch." But, it is added, he had not become particularly pious in his choice of words, for after "taking an active part in the services and listening attentively to the sermon, he would shock the faithful on his way out by expressing aloud to himself the belief that the minister was a damned poor or a damned good preacher. None of the sisters had the courage to remonstrate with him on his expressions as to the merits or demerits of the sermon."

So far as is known, Old Hutch joined no church, but lived as a sort of religious free lance, going where he pleased and saying what he pleased. The hand of welcome was always stretched out to him. His contributions were handsome. He denounced religious bigotry and as vigorously assailed those who set up a noisy clamor against Christianity. He seemed to have no fixed ideas other than that man should continue groping, for, he declared, all progress has been due to such search for truth; religion grew out of spiritual groping, just as scientific groping brought about the steam engine, sanitation and our knowledge of electricity, the laws of gravitation, and the circulation of the blood. Old Hutch was exceedingly tolerant and open minded for those days.

For some time after his interest in religious matters had been stirred, Hutch was more silent and uncommunicative than ever. The Pit was puzzled, and opinion was divided. Some contended that his religion was nothing more than a new fad, while many others believed that he had in truth been "washed in the blood."

XV

The Wizard Fails

THE eyes of all big plungers were constantly trained upon the Wheat King. Not for an instant did they fail to catalogue his every move and gesture. By a few operators he was now fiercely hated. By all he was genuinely feared. Yet a feeling was somehow permeating the markets, a feeling vague and intangible, that his star was paling. He seemed to have reached the apex of his speculative glory and was now hovering there insecurely, as if awaiting the dire fate of so many historic plungers—the lightning-fast tumble into obscurity.

Hutch studied the faces of his antagonists with quick penetrating eyes, eyes that at times became mocking. He knew that his dangers had multiplied, that in the future he must exercise even greater skill and cunning than required in the past. He knew, too, that he was under a heavy strain, mental and physical. His lean, unsmiling face was taking on deeper lines, and his body was growing weary; but still he was restless and combative, eager to be on with his schemes.

On the very first business day of the year 1889, a series of bear raids burst forth and continued until prices had been considerably depressed. This fitted in happily with the plans of the Wheat King, who sought once more to gather up immense holdings at low prices with a view to dictating values later on. When he believed the hour had arrived, he took hold of the market and bought heavily, being aided by the fact that four other capitalists had also enrolled on the bull side and were some twenty million bushels long. At the same time there was a threatened corner in the Milwaukee market in which Hutch was suspected of having a hand. This influenced Chicago prices in his favor.

Forces opposing the dictator were larger than he had counted upon, however, and, in the short period of sixty days his structure began to totter. One raid followed another, until he was forced to sell his wheat at a lower price than he had paid, and to join in with the bears as a matter of precaution and self protection. For a time he appeared to be pretty well beaten. He was heckled with quips tossed out by the more daring; he flared back at them in a fire of fury; he became intolerant of some of his close associates and intolerable to every one he encountered. He even let himself become involved in a dispute with Miss Fanny Blinn, the "woman wizard" who had created a system for beating the market, and who had thus drawn international notoriety. He neglected his duties long enough to prove the weakness of her system and finally caused it to go to smash, after she had challenged him to a market duel.

A short rest. Much sleep. A little reading and meditation. Long walks in the night. And once again his market balance and his titanic energy returned. Early in March he launched a new campaign of some magnitude, offering to buy all the wheat available at fixed figures. Prices were forced upward in quick, jerky movements amid wild excitement and rumors of a corner. So dominant was he for a few days that his very appearance at the Pit was the signal for a flurry of buying. When prices kept mounting, some traders rushed to him and settled their accounts, allowing Hutch large profits.

To strengthen prices in Chicago he again began toying with outside markets. Predictions were heard of a wheat corner in St. Louis and another in Milwaukee. The genius was tossing out his nets rapidly, dazzling his weaker opponents, and once more the panic-stricken crowd anticipated dreadful results. In consternation many stampeded to cover.

Not so, however, with more powerful operators. This time they had visualized the probable course of events and had quietly switched their holdings from the May future to the July future; and then they had begun lambasting wheat, selling it down, down, lower and lower. In St. Louis the high price bubble burst with sensational results. John Jackson, president of the St. Louis Elevator Company, ended his worries by committing suicide. Prices in all markets crushed downward. Hutch's losses were immense.

Coming events were casting their shadows. The clouds were thickening. Nor was Hutch unmindful of the situation. He could see dangers and weigh them. There was no fear or timidity or want of confidence on his part. But the facts were indisputable. He had been tricked and outwitted. Likewise he had been out-generaled. This was something new, something to be studied and analyzed. Perhaps the turmoil of the Pit was disquieting him, disturbing his mental poise. He complained that it wasn't the same old Pit of a few years ago. Faces were changing, the crowd was larger and noisier. Methods were undergoing a sort of transition. Outside markets were not so easy to handle. The signs by which he had always been guided seemed so indistinct and confused. Yes, the Pit was different. He would remain away for a time, directing his campaign from without, and perhaps his thoughts and his plans would crystalize more clearly.

A steady stream of messenger boys raced back and forth from his office to the floor of the exchange for the next three weeks. Hutch met no one and talked to no one. His orders to his brokers, delivered by messenger, were brief and direct. They had the old snap.

He worked far into the night, poring over a mass of figures, tables of statistics, charts marking the course of prices in recent years, private reports from all sections of the globe where wheat is grown. Night after night he struggled with the conundrum, lonely and weary. Only in the early hours of the morning would he put aside the gloomy puzzle of world supply and demand and wend his way homeward for a few hours of sleep.

On one of these black mornings, after the police had left their posts Old Hutch was walking slowly out

Van Buren street, his collar turned high and his hat pulled low to shut out a thick wet fog that hung over the sleeping city.

Suddenly two shadowy forms slipped out of the fog bank and barred his path. A moment later the long, lean barrel of a six shooter was poked vigorously into his ribs.

Hutch did not resist. Up went his hands. He stood stock still and remained silent while the two hold-up men ransacked his pockets and relieved him of the small change he carried.

Then Old Hutch chuckled. And, to the utter astonishment of the thugs, the chuckle grew into a gale of laughter.

"Be quiet! What are you laughing at? You old fool!" growled one of his assailants.

"I was just thinking," Hutch mused, "that in all my career this is the first time I've ever been really cornered. I'm Old Hutch."

"My God!" groaned one of the pair, as they scurried off in the fog.

Hutch went on his way enjoying what to him seemed a stupendous joke.

The crowd in the Pit was catching on to some of the cunning tricks of the dictator. In former days, by a skillful arrangement of his forces, he was able to dump huge quantities of grain on the market, thus depressing prices. He would scatter through the Pit a number of brokers who were not on his regular staff. These men would buy in all the grain he sold and millions of bushels additional at low prices. But now when he attempted the trick, the crowd would start buying instead of selling, and prices would be forced higher instead of sagging to low levels. It materially weakened his position as well as his prestige.

To retrieve his waning power he felt that something new and startling was essential. So he made a daring stroke. He deliberately passed his trading cards out among the brokers, offering to buy all corn available at a certain figure. There could be no trickery about that. The crowd was puzzled and impressed.

At about the same time, a sensation was created by the announcement that an enormous cargo of wheat had been sent from Chicago to Uruguay by way of New Orleans. Again the crowd was on the run. Hutch tried in vain to follow up these advantages, but the skill of past years was lacking. One ingenious stroke followed another, each more original and surprising than the last. And yet each in turn failed to advance his scheme of a complete corner.

These ineffectual attempts to bull wheat brought new gibes, and at length he was derisively dubbed "The Sitting Bull." This cut deeply into the old man. He could not stand ridicule. He could not be satirized or scoffed at. He lost his composure completely, became sarcastic and biting, and in sharp, caustic words poured forth a stream of withering abuse that silenced the Pit. The poise with which he had dominated had at last left him forever. He was a different man, a ready fighter, surly, acrimonious, and voluble.

New enemies. Many of them. Old enemies on the alert and biding their time. Dangers increasing daily. Outside markets guarding their interests as never before. Millions of dollars ready and waiting to be tossed into the battle against Old Hutch, now regarded as the common enemy. Such was the situation as the year drew toward a close, a year replete with sensational price swings, due to the desultory pyrotechnics of the veteran plunger.

While the frenzied pits were bursting with excitement, and wild scenes were drawing crowds of spectators that had to be held in bounds by the police, a new scheme to trap Old Hutch was quietly incubating. No single man could be credited with charting the sinister course over which it was hoped to lure the Wheat King.

It was the composite work of a dozen active brains. The clique was headed by Cudahy, a sworn eternal enemy of the dictator, and ever alert to strike back in memory of the fierce financial battering he had sustained on several occasions.

A few years before, even one year before, Hutch could not have been drawn into the snare. He had always looked straight through such guile and market collusion. But this time he had been too busy, or the masquerade had been too disarming, or the bait too attractive.

Corn was chosen as the field of battle. The price had been made to appear too high. Hutch had sold short, and prices sagged, promising large profits. He sold more and more. Deeper and deeper he was beckoned into the trap. When he noticed that the corn market was as peaceful as if lulled by an opiate, he took no warning. Nor again, when he sensed an unusual tranquility and serenity on the part of his chief opponents, did he recognize that a storm was brewing.

Finally the giant trap was sprung. This time the dictator himself was the victim. He had sold corn down to thirty-three cents a bushel, sold it short in staggering volumes. Now the price began advancing. It ran up like the indicator on a scales. The coup had been a perfect success. The clique pressed its advantage. Corn almost doubled in price within a few days.

Old Hutch, the man who would be Wheat King, the genius who had caused the grain world to tremble when he thundered, "Step up to the captain," was at last struggling for breath, outraged, mortified, and shaken.

Where was his titanic strength? Why had his brain been clouded? Amid all the turmoil, all the battle of years, fighting in four pits at a time, he had been calm, fully master of himself when a crisis arose. His decisions had been well rounded, brilliant and cool, like polished ivory spheres. Yet on this occasion his mind had been misty. His magic touch was gone.

"Everything seemed so different," he complained to a friend, and his brow was furrowed with the puzzle.

The incredible news traveled like lightning; Old Hutch, whose big brain had encompassed the grain problems of every nation under the sun months in advance, who had fought and won a hundred battles in the Pit by reason of superior intellect, and whose physical bigness alone had exercised on the imagination of many a sort of almost overpowering fascination, had at last been compelled to admit defeat, bitter defeat, even if only temporary. Moreover, he was being forced to dig deep into his millions, as penance for his delinquency.

Nor was he alone in his losses. There were Lindblom and Singer and Baldwin and others who still believed in his genius and his power and who had trailed the mirage of low corn prices over the brink of ruin. Some of them came back; others remained in obscurity.

The corn trap was the first of two crushing events. The second came within a year.

Hutch recognized that the tide was turning from him. His small but sturdy army of followers were dropping off one by one. His opinions, once deemed invaluable, carried little influence and failed to cause more than a ripple in prices. E. Nelson Blake, for years an important figure on the exchange, left Chicago to make his home elsewhere and in a farewell interview characterized Hutch as "The Old Man of the Sea," whom the grain markets had on their backs. This phrase seized the imagination and grew into criticism, which in turn became bitter denunciation.

For a few weeks Hutch did no trading. He sought to regain his market balance. He passed some time in a verbal duel with leaders of the Wheat Growers' Federation, which had met and made plans to corner the surplus wheat of the nation. The plan as outlined in resolutions embodied an agreement that farmers would not sell their wheat under a certain fixed price, which was well over its actual value.

"A lot of simpletons," Hutch declared. "If I cannot corner the market how can these ridiculous organizers expect to do so when they know nothing of the game? I give their scheme one month."

He was too liberal, for in seven days the farm plan collapsed and drove prices much lower. Sensing that prices were somewhat above normal, farmers had deemed it well to sell their wheat right then while the talk of a farmers' corner was on. So many of them did sell that prices tumbled. Thus ended another price-fixing scheme.

Hutch then amused himself by joining in the battle against the bucket shop evil, a fight that spanned two decades and in which the exchange spent millions of dollars. The campaign against the bucketeers was launched by W. T. Baker, "Bucket Shop Baker," the only man who ever served five terms as president of the Board of Trade, and who died in 1903, two years before the famous supreme court decision holding that there were property rights in quotations. That decision sounded the death knell of the bucket shop evil. Baker died believing his battle a failure.

To keep the bucketeers from stealing the Pit quotations, all entrances to the exchange save one were barred. Still the outlaws thrived. Next the use of telephones in the exchange was prohibited. And still the evil continued.

"Well," Hutch announced one day, "I've found the leak." He pointed to a messenger boy idling near a window inside the exchange. Every now and then the boy would remove his cap; replace it; run his fingers through his hair; take a few steps forward and then a few backward.

From the window of a nearby building a clerk with field glasses was reading the silent code of the messenger and in this way stealing the legitimate Pit quotations for distribution to bucket shops throughout the country.

"Let's soap the windows," said Hutch, and next day all windows of the trading floor were heavily coated. In ten days a hundred powerful bucket shops, all in full blossom, found it expedient to close their doors.

Early in the year 1890 Hutch threw himself once more into the swift, shifting pageant of pit life. In the following months his picturesque figure darted back and forth across the stage. He must have known that the last act of his great speculative drama was approaching, for he cuffed dreams and verse and pleasure into the background. Every ounce of energy was thrown into the work. His old genius would flare up for a few days, and one brilliant coup would follow another. But to his great distress all were too short-lived to be of any real financial consequence.

After a time, as his victories narrowed, he seemed to become rasher, less patient of the normal obstacles, more and more anxious to lash the Pit with his remaining millions and toss in the sponge. Whereas his major speculations had always been founded on logic of events, he was now inclined to resort to sheer daring.

His quarrels with the bull leaders and the bear leaders recurred with greater frequency, and his dislike of Bloom grew into an obsession. Finally he laid a new trap for that plunger who, like the hero of a melodrama, rushed onto the floor at the last second with an armful of securities valued at a million dollars and stemmed the tide, just in time to save the remnant of the fortune he had brought out of the Franco-Prussian war.

Up to the first three weeks in autumn Hutch had made some progress in his major effort to bull wheat. It had seemed on the surface to be an era of advancing prices. The signing of the McKinley tariff law helped the general situation. Politicians were talking prosperity, and bankers were parroting their words, knowing full well, however, that the financial structure was teetering more ominously each day. Now and then a straw pointed the direction of the wind. Here and there a bank closed its doors. Sawyer, Wallace and Company of New York failed for two millions. They had had many branch offices. Hutch had acted as their broker. He took his heavy loss with a smile and bought more wheat. And prices climbed.

Early in November Wall Street began to tremble. Money was getting distressingly tight. Stocks had reached dangerous ground and began slumping; then of a sudden they crashed to sickening levels, as Wall Street fought frantically to extricate itself from the ruins. Pessimistic reports poured out of the East in a deluge. Then from other districts they began clattering in over the wires. Signs all pointed to a national panic.

Wheat began slipping, slipping; a market crisis was impending. Old Hutch knew it. But he did not rush to cover by selling his wheat. Instead he resumed buying on a gigantic scale, pouring more and more of his fortune into the sickly market.

"We must hold the wheat market!" he shouted above the din.

"If wheat smashes, Chicago will have a panic." And he drove his brokers to a frenzy of activity.

"The man is mad!" some one called. "Nothing can save wheat. The panic is on."

Hutch shot back:

"Yes, money and courage can save wheat and save La Salle Street. Come on, boys!" he roared. "We're fighting now for the common good. We're fighting to save the market. Let's whoop her up!"

And the warrior beckoned the crowd to follow as he rushed into the center of the Pit. The thrilling old spirit of loyalty caught part of the crowd in the throat. Many veterans of past deals followed Hutch into the Pit and helped dam up the flood. This support definitely saved the day and prevented an immediate panic that might have had far reaching consequences in Chicago.

Hutch left the market plugged with his millions, hoping for better conditions later that would permit him to withdraw. But fate had written otherwise.

On the morning of November fifteenth stupendous news shook the financial world. The great London house of Baring Brothers, a Gibraltar of finance second only to the Bank of England, was on the verge of ruin. Then came other reports fast and furious; failures in

Philadelphia; bank runs in New York and Boston. A great cotton firm in the south collapsed; then the large house of A. E. Bateman of New York.

Once more wheat flooded the market in millions of bushels. And Old Hutch bought, bought, bought. For three full days he supported the falling market, buying with utter disregard of personal consequences. Finally the storm subsided. And to the surprise of the financial world not a single failure of consequence had been allowed to occur in Chicago.

By reason of his lofty deed, his loyalty to Chicago and to the market, the Wheat King had fed most of his remaining millions back into the Pit from which they had come . . .

Old Hutch was a remnant.

XVI

Adrift

BLACK shadows of defeat were lowering like a velvet curtain, shutting him in, choking him. To one of his sensitive temperament the sensation was hideous, a torture to the soul. His imaginative mind was filled with frightful visions of the future. He confided to closest friends that he could see naught but darkness ahead.

Tangled nerves were punishing Old Hutch. Nerves strained and shattered by years of torment in the Pit. Nerves that had been twisted, drawn tight, and tied like the strings of a violin, only to be snapped back into a tangle. To his distress, reports were current that out of deference to the wishes of his family he was to quit speculation and that a conservator had been threatened to prevent dissipation of his fortune, which had shrunk nineteen millions of dollars.

Flaming with indignation he branded the reports as deliberate falsehoods.

Edward Pardridge, the biggest and most picturesque bear the Pit ever knew, went to Old Hutch and sought to commiserate with him.

"I sincerely hope," he said in a tone that to Hutch seemed tinged with sarcasm, "I sincerely hope that you will not need a conservator."

"Conservator!" shouted the outraged Hutch in a violence of passion. "Conservator! Mind these words: You will need a receiver before I need a conservator."

Pardridge, who in turn was convulsed with anger, blustered away. He had accepted a challenge.

A bitter duel in the Pit, the last dramatic duel Hutch ever fought, soon was in progress. For a time the honors swayed back and forth. At length they settled upon Hutch. In one month the great Pardridge had been clearly defeated. He was obliged to ask creditors to accept notes until he could turn real estate into money. The *Herald* wrote: "Hutchinson's operations are amazing. Pardridge, without meaning it, gave him mortal offense. A campaign against Pardridge cost the latter half a million and severely humbled him. Hutch is as keen as ten years ago. Signs of age are gone. To-day he commands the markets in wheat, corn, and oats."

This temporary command was nothing more than the final brilliant stroke of a master strategist. Hutch knew as much, and so did the other big operators. Accordingly he relinquished his grip, slowly, and with skillful maneuvering, thus salvaging what fortune remained.

Meantime he had had the good judgment and foresight to settle upon Mrs. Hutchinson and his youngest son, W. I. Hutchinson, about one million dollars in the form of a trust fund, retaining a few hundred thousand dollars for his own use.

He was growing desperately unhappy. With an imagination that could live every life, feel every pang of pain, his idle hours were wretched and filled with anxiety. For days he moved about as if in a dream. He confided to friends that this dreary, troubled world held no more fascination. For him the sun had lost its glory and the stars their charm.

He spent one entire day in a little room high over the trading floor, listening to the dim roar of the Pit. He spent that night on the low slung balcony, staring down into the yawning Pit below, dreaming of the past and dreading the future. Then in the early morning hours the vanquished Wheat King silently slipped out of the city and left no word behind.

News of his disappearance caused a great sensation. The Pit was overwhelmed. For a time it looked as if panic would sweep the market. As the name of Hutchinson had always been associated with gigantic deals, it was only natural that rumors should begin to fly. Perhaps the vanquished Wheat King was insolvent and had left debts totaling millions. Perhaps a big financial disaster would be the result. Hourly such a turn of events was expected by the frightened traders. Meantime the wires buzzed with messages to all cities in the country to be on the lookout for the picturesque old plunger.

But those who knew Hutch best had no fears of a financial disaster. His loyalty to the city and to the Street had been shown on too many occasions. He was incapable of saddling his own losses onto others.

George F. Bishop gave a dinner, attended by the city's leading financiers, as an expression of confidence in the integrity of the missing Wheat King, and this resolution was adopted: "As associates for many years of B. P. Hutchinson in all the vicissitudes of business on the Board of Trade, the subscribers desire to express to him and to the public their appreciation of his character as a business man, and to say to the world that he has for thirty years stood for the very highest type of honor and integrity in all transactions between man and man. And he does not and never did owe a dollar which he did not pay."

As he drifted about from city to city, reading the scareheads on the nation-wide search to determine his whereabouts, Hutch must have chuckled over the turmoil created by his sudden departure.

Even after the Pit learned that he was quite solvent and that he had left his finances ship-shape, the eagerness for some kind of a statement from him was in no way lessened, and detectives and newspaper reporters flitted about the country in the wake of every vague and intangible clew.

At length he was met face to face by an intrepid reporter who had dogged his trail to Boston.

"Mr. Hutchinson, I want a statement from you."

"Well, you can't have it. Get out of here."

"But I'm an honest reporter and will write only what you say."

"Good Lord!" exclaimed Hutch. "Sit down and let's talk. This is indeed an experience. I've never before met an honest reporter. But why do you want a statement from me?"

"Because it will be the big event of the day from the standpoint of national interest."

"All right. Go ahead. But I'll answer only questions that appeal to me."

"Why did you disappear from Chicago?"

"I think Tecumseh Sherman and Robert E. Lee were the two greatest generals in the world. . . . Now mind. Quote me exactly."

"Do you expect to return to Chicago?"

"I think prospects for a wheat crop were never better."

"What do you think of the present value of wheat, Mr. Hutchinson?"

"It is worth the money."

"How about corn? Is it a good purchase right now?" the reporter asked with intense earnestness.

"Young man, you have been speculating. And you're seeking market information. Don't blush and stammer. But just leave the market alone. It is no business for a careless reporter."

"How long will you remain in the East, Mr. Hutchinson?"

"Literature is the greatest blessing of mankind and the most glorious solace in times of uncertainty."

"Have you retired from active speculation?"

"Bob Ingersoll is by far the best preacher in the country to-day."

"Do your recent losses really total millions?"

"Grover Cleveland will be the next president of the United States. Daniel Webster was the greatest man this state of Massachusetts ever knew, and, as a lawyer, Rufus Choate was incomparable. Old Cornelius Vanderbilt was the brightest business man in the country's history."

Hutch paused.

"You speak of the genius of Ingersoll, Mr. Hutchinson. They say you recently got religion. What do you consider follows death?"

"Sleep. Sleep. Eternal sleep and happiness."

"And what do you think of money?"

"The most despicable word in the English language. The sorrow it brings is without limit. Maybe some day enlightened mankind will somehow avoid the tortures of the present money system. Every man should pursue an art or an ambition without the necessary consciousness of money."

"Now returning to religion——"

"I don't care to talk religion further. I've said I am not concerned whether a man is a Catholic or a Methodist; a Baptist or a Universalist. If he is a man, that satisfies me. My religion is Tom Paine's.

"Now, young man, this momentous interview is at an end. And, say," he called as an afterthought, "you had better not dabble in corn. Reporting is much simpler; your blunders die and are buried with each edition."

Hutch wanted nothing so much as to be left alone. He studied long and hard over the problem of how to exclude himself from every one and at the same time be in close proximity to the markets. Finally he reached a conclusion. He would go to New York. That was the place. He would lose himself among its millions. He would live alone in the very heart of Wall Street, a street that always had many recluses.

He rented a tiny office, had telephones and other wire facilities installed, and then closed the door to every one.

Living in this Wall Street solitariness he gave big market orders in both stocks and grains, influenced the course of prices, matured several small corners, and from time to time distributed punishment among erstwhile comrades of the West. All of this he did before it was even discovered that he was holding forth in New York.

In this solitude Old Hutch seemed to grieve less over his immense financial losses in the Pit than over the good-natured jibes of wheat brokers, which had fallen upon his ears during the final months in the Pit. He learned from time to time that Chicago would welcome him back; that without his leadership the market had become faltering and uncertain. But he could not think of returning. He could think only of the facetious horse play of a few brokers who had staged an impromptu festival around the Pit, laughing at what they deemed a good humored jibe at "The Sitting Bull," but which Old Hutch regarded as unpardonable ridicule.

Brooding over the incident he concluded that Pardridge must have been the instigator. Perhaps he had not punished the rascal sufficiently. From New York he could give the big bear one more thorough trouncing, before he even knew what was happening. Then he would be satisfied. He would feel that his slate was clean. He could quit for good. Thus did the old man now devote his flagging genius to repeated strokes of revenge.

By observing closely the course of prices late in the summer, Hutch knew that Pardridge had become heavily short. At the "charmed hour" Hutch began to buy, feeling the market out carefully as he proceeded, so as to avoid quick upturns and subsequent suspicions. In the course of time, Pardridge discovered with great surprise that he was in difficulty. But this surprise turned to consternation when he determined that the vanquished King was still his foe and had once more proved his mettle and his superior generalship in the Pit.

A record of the incident includes this comment: "Pardridge's losses were estimated at three quarters of a million dollars. Ream, Lindblom, and Roche were also among the victims. While it was acknowledged that a New York syndicate headed the bull movement, it was believed that the directing force was B. P. Hutchinson, and this theory proved correct."

Old Hutch kept wholly aloof from social relations in New York. He slept every night in his tiny Wall Street office, a swivel chair serving as bed. In a few weeks, despite all measures to the contrary, intruders began annoying him. On one pretext or another they would call. Some were courteously persistent and chatted of things they believed would intrigue the interest of Old Hutch. He soon found his solitude once more slipping away.

"Tell me," asked a venturesome broker coaxingly, "how do you like being a New Yorker?"

"Don't care to discuss it," was the tart response.

"Different from Chicago?"

"Yep—like me—Chicago's gone to seed."

That was a long conversation for the former Wheat King.

His desire to be alone, a desire that became almost an obsession in the period immediately following his big failures, finally led him to desert Wall Street and speculation. Once more he dropped completely from sight, and the Street knew of him no longer. His disappearance again proved a mystery to all save his immediate family.

This time when Hutch slipped into new surroundings, he changed his attire, adopting the most unobtrusive of garments. His western manner of dress, which in recent years had become more garish, with his Dolly Varden vest of a highly ornamental pattern, butternut trousers, and orange colored shirt, all topped by a tall silk hat, had made him an object of curiosity wherever he went in the east. This regalia was exchanged for a simple sack suit of black.

For a long time nothing was heard of Old Hutch. Efforts of friends to locate him through his family were unavailing. Many believed him to be dead. In the Pit his leadership had been divided among many.

Later on a special writer in the *New York Herald* created wide interest among readers with a series of stories concerning the pronouncements of a philosopher with a wide and mellow perspective of life, whom he had by chance discovered, but whose name and place of residence were concealed. The words of this philosopher on religion, history, war, and economics glittered with wisdom. No one could guess who he was, and the writer took pains to conceal the man who was proving such a source of copy.

One day the writer was acting as host to a Chicago visitor. The westerner had been keenly interested in the views expressed by the unknown philosopher, and when the suggestion of a visit was advanced he leaped at the opportunity. Together the two men made their way toward the Brooklyn Bridge. Arriving under the western approach to the bridge, they entered a small store containing a meager stock of notions.

In an armchair in one corner sat an old man. He was surrounded by stacks of books on almost every conceivable subject. He arose and came around the counter.

The Chicago man took a quick step forward, stared for a moment, and then in a tone of astonishment cried out:

"Why, that's Old Hutch!"

The fallen Wheat King smiled and put out his hand.

"Yes, I am Old Hutch." Then after a moment he

added: "All I have asked is that I be left alone. But now once more my prize—solitude—has been stolen. I am discovered."

After fading out of Wall Street, Hutch had drifted about the city for a few days incognito. At noon one day he chanced to be passing the little notion store just at the moment that the sheriff was offering it to the highest bidder, as a consequence of the financial mishaps of one Max Schoenberg, whose name was emblazoned across the windows. Hutch bought the store, paid cash, and did not trouble to remove the name of the defunct predecessor. He had deemed this an ideal hiding place, a haven where he might read and dream and meditate undisturbed. Now he had again been jerked back into the public spotlight against his will.

He was urged over and over again to write his memoirs, but bluntly brushed aside all such proposals with the comment that "they would display nothing but dismal failure."

He did consent to write for the *North American Review* a prophetic article in which he asserted that never again would there be a large and successful corner in wheat. It was a sound, true prophecy grounded in logic. He declared, too, that prices could never be controlled, regardless of funds available.

"Grain is a commodity every man has a right to buy and sell. He has a right to buy it as low as he can and sell it as high as he can. But he must always buy and sell at the market price. This market price is the universal price all over the world on any given day. And no man or combination of men can stand up against it. They may take measures to influence it. But they cannot positively control it. It is too mighty, too immense. We can influence the waterpower of Niagara; but let us find the man or men who can stop the cataract!"

He wrote that speculation would always be necessary in the safe and judicious distribution of the crop over the world.

"In plentiful times men are apt to waste flour. When there is a short crop then speculation in the form of capital—provident, thrifty capital, the daughter of economy and the sworn enemy of waste—steps in, takes the precious wheat, and says: 'Now each of you inhabitants of the planet can have your share. But these are times of death, and in order to keep you from using more than your proper share the price must be raised.' This is a wise law of trade. Make the loaf small and dear, if the crop is short. Then no one will waste it. Diamonds are small and dear, and no one wastes them. But a man can fling diamonds into the sea with a better conscience than he can waste bread when the world is hungry. . . .

"We do not really know how wise capital is in dealing with food until we put an extreme case. Suppose there were but one bushel of wheat in the world, and a parcel of hungry men were fighting to eat it, and thus ignorantly destroy the future food crops of the universe. Capital steps in and lays its hands on the bag and says: 'The price of this bushel is five hundred millions of dollars.' This disperses the small hungry mob and saves humanity in its total. That bushel of wheat, if really the only surviving bushel, would be worth far more than Manhattan Island with every building on it full of costly merchandise. This is an extreme case, but the principle holds good. Capital guards against waste and protects the future of the people. And speculation is only another name for capital in active motion."

In the course of time Old Hutch was brought back to Chicago by his family. Gradually his health failed; a conservator was appointed in order to avoid the possibility of a return to the Pit, an event that induced his erstwhile rivals to sigh with relief. But they need not have worried. Hutch was through with the Pit. He had dreamed a grand dream—a dream of permanent rulership over wheat prices in the world market—the Chicago Pit. He felt that fate had snatched away his one big opportunity. Meantime increased production and, more important still, the revision of marketing machinery, had forever made such ambition a sheer fantasy.

Queer tales have been woven about the later life of Old Hutch. Most of them are pure fabrication, or rumor so oft-repeated as to take on the cloak of truth. There is the story that for years after his great corner and his subsequent failure Hutch was reduced to poverty and mental darkness; that his bent and bony figure might be seen wandering the streets about the Pit, always carrying in his hand a lighted lantern. Then there is the tale that he suffered from a recurring illusion that all the wheat in the world was being piled high upon him, crushing him, smothering out his life. Another legend, equally grotesque, told how he cried out in his sleep each night against the specters of those whom he had beaten down to defeat in the early days of his forward sweep to power. The most persistent of the legends is the one crediting him with having deliberately and systematically fed his millions back into the Pit, so that he might die a comparatively poor man.

All are without any apparent basis of fact.

XVII

Heir to the Throne

MANY eager, trembling hands reached out in vain for the coveted, elusive crown of Wheat King, after the passing of Old Hutch. Some craved the wealth and power which it brought; others sought the glory. A few hungered for revenge. But one by one the strong contenders fell by the wayside, most of them finding that their ambition was only an illusion born of vanity. The crown remained where the genius had dropped it.

And then came young Joe Leiter, son of the merchant prince; young Joe with his winning smile, his flashing eye, and his vast amount of good sense. He was big and strong, bold as a hawk, and had a burning desire to be Wheat King.

He was born in Chicago in 1868, graduated from Harvard, and then traveled widely. It had been the plan of his father, Levi Z. Leiter, to place him in charge of his immense real estate holdings, and, accordingly, he advanced one million dollars at the proper time to be used as working capital.

But Joe had no taste for the prosaic profession of land agent. He thrived best on color and drama and swift action. He had listened to the roar of the Pit, and it had stirred him like the blast of a bugle. Night and day the music of the trading ring kept beating in his veins. The call became irrepressible and irresistible, and finally this chap of thirty plunged headlong into his great adventure, with a recklessness that snatches victory out of the jaws of danger. At first he was regarded only as a mathematical genius and an accurate observer. Later it was seen that he had the stuff of a hero in him.

Old Hutch lived to see the inception of the Leiter deal as well as its cruel and bitter denouement.

"Mind you, he is a bright boy, a boy with plenty of fortitude," Hutch had said, when the campaign was well under way. "But," he repeated, "it can't be done again. The market is too big, too immense. We shall never see another complete corner." Then he added these prophetic words: "And God pity young Leiter when he has the corpse of the deal on his hands!"

Again the prophecy of the vanquished Wheat King rang true, for it was indeed the corpse, a hideous gigantic corpse spread out over railroad yards and standing upright in towering elevators, that filled Leiter's days with feverish anxiety and his nights with sleepless hours of torment.

At the outset of his speculative drama Leiter had tossed a part of his million into the Pit and had lost. He speculated again and lost. Then he made a third attempt and came out with a neat pile. By this stroke he was thrilled, bubbling over with confidence, ready and eager to push his luck to the limit.

Then began his attempted corner, the longest single deal in history. It was in 1897. The wheat market had been colorless during the first few months of the year. Like a skilled veteran of speculation the boy plunger had been studying world crop conditions, probable needs of various nations, and the probable exports of countries producing a surplus. As an analyst he showed marked ability.

By the middle of July prices began to dance about, rising and receding, rising and receding. But each rise was greater than the preceding one, and each decline fell short of its previous mark. Before August slipped away the air was thick with rumors associating various big financial interests with a huge deal. The "syndicate" was reputed to hold sixteen million bushels of wheat, corn, and oats. None of the big traders believed the Leiter boy could have any material part in such an enormous campaign.

But the Leiter boy went right on buying wheat, or rather contracts for wheat that would have to be delivered to him in Chicago during the month of December. Failure to deliver would permit Leiter to dictate prices at which contracts could be settled.

Meantime it became apparent that he had chosen a most propitious time for his attempted corner. From an economic standpoint he was in an exceptionally strong position. The importing countries of Europe had produced two hundred million bushels of wheat less than the year before. Reserves everywhere were low. Among exporting countries, the United States alone showed any surplus. To buy this surplus was to make Europe pay the holder's own price for it—theoretically. And such was the ambitious aim of the daring speculator.

A vital part of the plan was to keep stocks of wheat in Chicago reasonably low. This would prevent the big shorts from making delivery to Leiter during the month of December. Thus he could push the price sky high, and with his millions in profits buy more physical wheat to withhold from Europe. Late in November he began sending wheat out of Chicago, first in carloads, then in trainloads. On the last day of the month, by reason of his efforts, exports were the largest in the history of American wheat trade.

It was the middle of December before the Pit knew definitely that Leiter alone was in the saddle, that the "boy wonder" had apparently cornered the market in December wheat.

At this time another startling discovery was made. It was found that on the opposite end of the Leiter deal was old P. D. Armour, founder of the Armour millions, now savage and uncompromising, flinty and a bit sinister, a man who neither asked nor gave quarter. He was short millions of bushels of wheat which, by his contracts, he was obliged to deliver to Leiter in Chicago during December.

Here indeed was drama enough for any upstart. The grain world looked on agog. Never had a new contender to market leadership dared to oppose the Armour millions and the Armour skill by entering into a clean cut deal. Under the circumstances what would the Leiter boy do? Would he be frightened out? Would he throw up his hands and ask for mercy? Would his big speculative bubble burst? Every one anticipated such eventualities.

But young Leiter was made of different stuff.

"I have the old fox!" he fairly shouted in glee. "I have him! He's literally hog tied. Now let him face the music. He has contracted to deliver the wheat. He must do so or settle at my price."

Peedy Armour scowled and grumbled incoherently as the brave words of the dare-devil were repeated to him. He was accustomed to rough tactics, but not on the part of a rank amateur. He went straight to Leiter.

"Young feller, what's ailing you?"

"Not a thing, Mr. Armour. You've contracted to deliver a little wheat, I believe. Since you can't deliver the wheat you'll have to settle."

"I will not settle!" Armour stormed.

"Oh, yes you will."

"I won't!"

"What will you do then?"

"I'll deliver the wheat!"

"That's impossible. Ridiculous," said Joe Leiter. Then he laughed, laughed outright in the face of the great Armour. That was a blunder. He never should have laughed. But he was young and confident and bold.

Peedy Armour's heavy jaw closed with a click, and he walked rapidly away, his mind made up.

"We'll see," he murmured. "We'll see."

The month was December, the most difficult month of the year for getting wheat to Chicago. There was wheat to be had in the northwest and in Canada, but at this season the Great Lakes freeze over and navigation closes. Already the ice was thickening up a bit, and the big inland seas were cleared of craft. Lake insurance had expired. Any skipper headstrong enough to put out to sea did so at the owner's risk.

Such was the situation that faced Peedy Armour, a nettling situation "brought about by an unreasonable, smart aleck young pirate." His wrath was flaming high when he returned to his office and began dispatching telegrams to hundreds of agents scattered about the northwest. The gist of the messages was:

"Buy up all the wheat available. Concentrate it immediately at Duluth."

Then Armour started gathering a fleet of lake vessels. He chartered a few here and a few there until he had a score or more. He personally assumed the insurance risk, guaranteeing to return each ship in good condition or pay for the damage incurred.

His next step was to charter a fleet of sturdy tugs. Within twenty-four hours the tugs began plowing their

way through the ice of the Duluth harbor, fighting to
open up a narrow lane along which the big carriers
might move with some degree of safety. He engaged
extra crews of hard headed seamen, rugged fellows
who were fearless in the face of a hazardous task. He
kept them struggling incessantly against the enemy—
the rapidly forming ice—and paid handsome bonuses
for exceptional service. All night long powerful search-
lights played like streams of fire across the icy stretches
of the harbor, as the shrieking tugs pounded back and
forth from dock to open sea.

Meantime, other tugs were busy smashing through
the ice of the Fort William Harbor, preparatory to the
dangerous sailing of wheat-laden vessels from that
point.

At last the fleet began crawling toward Chicago,
each boat being conveyed by tugs that crashed a narrow passage through the grumbling ice. Nearly a dozen
boats arrived, unloaded a cargo of a million bushels,
and hoping to conquer the ice once more, raced back
to Duluth for another load.

It was soon learned with some amazement that the
water lane had been broken wide open; an unbelievable
accomplishment. More boats bearing wheat came bel-

lowing into Chicago under black billows of smoke, and in a frenzy of haste to start the homeward journey again.

Railroads now were likewise making deliveries for Armour; his giant elevators, shells that towered high like slender skyscrapers, were slowly filling up. But these containers were unused to loading from boats; their construction was intended for rail service. So the process was proving extremely awkward. Armour needed more space and needed it quickly.

Without a moment's delay he ordered the construction of a huge warehouse, engaged hundreds of carpenters and common laborers, kept three shifts working right around the clock, and in three weeks the enormous reservoir was completed.

Leiter got his wheat. It poured in on him in unending streams. Notices of delivery on the December future contracts flew about thick and fast. As the month closed Chicago elevators held some ten million bushels of wheat, nearly all of which had been delivered to young Joe Leiter.

Peedy Armour, a fighter of the old school, had kept his contract. His job was done. He smiled and rubbed his hands together in satisfaction.

As wheat flooded into the city, prices began to tumble. But Joe Leiter did not turn and run. Instead he accepted all the wheat on the contracts he held and paid for it.

"Despondent! Certainly I am not despondent," he replied to a question, smilingly. "Why I never was so confident in my life. You just watch wheat!"

Leiter went into the new year with the corpse on his hands. It soon grew to fifteen million bushels. He bought heavily of May wheat futures, confident that his position was secure and that he was complete master of the situation. In some quarters he was being referred to as the new Wheat King, the successor to Old Hutch.

His outlook, however, was anything but rosy. Dangers were growing.

But Fate offered him one more chance. He had marked the price of wheat up from eighty-five cents to a dollar and nine cents. The world had begun to clamor for wheat. The war between the United States and Spain came on as opportunely for the deal as though it had been carefully devised by Leiter himself. Europe suddenly turned panic stricken over a vision of American wheat shipments cut off by Spanish men-of-war. France suspended her wheat import duties of thirty-six cents a bushel. Other countries followed.

By the tenth day of May, young Joe Leiter, by reason of fundamental conditions, stood to cash in a profit of eighty-five cents a bushel, making his total profit seven millions of dollars.

But still he held on unrelentingly. Wheat, he believed, would go much higher.

"Mankind will always dig out hidden stores of wheat if the price is high enough," commented Old Hutch. "Look out."

The price kept rising, but with each five cent advance, wheat now began to appear as if by magic. The northwest was sweeping its bins. Russia ate rye and emptied her mills of wheat. Argentine scraped the floor and following the lead of India, dispatched wheat laden ships to this country. And to top it all, a new American crop was at hand.

In spite of these developments, Leiter's opportunity for immense profits still remained. May wheat climbed up and touched the high point of a dollar and eighty-five cents a bushel. But the "boy wonder" stood poised on his mountain of success wholly oblivious to the coming disaster. He utterly disregarded all the glaring danger signals.

Wheat destiny moves swiftly, and the dismal windup of the Leiter deal was near at hand. With his gi-

gantic corpse to be disposed of Leiter had spent periods
of sleepless uncertainty awaiting the approach of May.
As he had anticipated, that month drove away his cares
and brought his big opportunity. Then came the blunder, perhaps the biggest blunder in the history of the
Pit. For some unknown reason Leiter suddenly determined to carry the corpse over into June, an impossible
and foolhardy undertaking.

Of a sudden wheat poured into Chicago from all sections. The golden streams became golden rivers. No one
could stem the tide. It came in boats and in trains and
in wagons. Leiter fought bravely for a time, fought like
a hero. But the corpse, which once offered staggering
profits, had now become a Frankenstein's monster. It
sought the destruction of its creator.

On June thirteenth the paralyzing blow fell with
dazzling swiftness. The deal collapsed, tumbled pros-
trate across a Pit of frantic brokers fighting like mad
men.

The boy plunger was through.

His father came to the rescue. The elder Leiter was
forced to sacrifice much choice real estate and gilt
edged securities. Three years later, when all accounts
were settled, it was estimated that the "ride through the

Pit" had carved a nine million dollar hole in the Leiter fortune.

Old Peedy Armour sent his photograph to young Leiter, bearing the scrawled inscription:

"With Best Regards."

Later Armour took over for disposal the physical wheat that had been assembled in the deal.

"When the operator overdoes things," said Old Hutch, "the penalty follows closely. He must know how to handle the corpse. I once figured that under no circumstances could more than three million bushels of wheat be tendered me on my contracts for September. On the last day of the month, over and above the three million came three hundred thousand bushels. And it was just this, and not the other, that seemed excessive. Wheat from St. Louis and from Detroit met that day and poured down on my shoulders!"

In spite of his enormous failure, Joe Leiter was looked upon as a hero, and to this day is so regarded by old timers familiar with the deal. It happened that his campaign came at a time when depression prevailed and spirits were low. The well-timed boom in wheat carried all other farm prices upward, and this in turn stimulated business generally. Farmers were extremely grateful to Leiter, and it was asserted over and over again that had he passed the hat among Kansas farmers, they alone would gladly have made up his losses.

But Europe had been incensed over the deal, and news of the collapse was received in England with great rejoicing. One London paper expressed the sentiment of all when it said:

"If the principal mover in this war against mankind is beggared by his greed, the retribution is well merited."

Curiously, the attempted corner was just ten years after the big and successful Hutchinson corner, and just ten years before the Patten deal, which is erroneously referred to as a corner. James A. Patten, always the merchant and investor rather than the plunger, never cornered wheat and never attempted a corner. Instead he predicted the forthcoming shortage after a long and careful study of fundamental conditions, bought immense quantities, urging every one he met to do likewise, held the wheat until prices were sky high, and then sold it. After he had sold out, prices went still higher. This was indisputable evidence that fundamental conditions and not manipulation had put prices up. Incidentally, the vast purchases by Patten kept wheat from leaving the country and likewise prevented a wheat famine in America later on. Patten was a business man and investor, first, last, and all the time, and could not properly be classed with the old time plungers that stormed across the last half of the nineteenth century and wrote Wheat Pit history with bank rolls that made the financial world dizzy.

A sharp echo of the disastrous Leiter deal, thirty years after its inception, was heard in Chicago in 1927. Nobility paraded into a court room as dissatisfied heirs of the late Levi Z. Leiter, and began fighting over a thirty million dollar prize. The chief aim of the noble descendants of Leiter was to oust Joseph as a trustee and from the management of the estate. Heading the group was Leiter's titled sister, Lady Marguerite Hyde, Countess of Suffolk and Berks. Lady Cynthia Moseley and Lady Alexandra Metcalf, the Baroness of Ravensdale, daughters of Lord Curzon, also sought to remove Leiter, who on his side had the support of his sister, Mrs. Nancy Carver Campbell, wife of Colonel Colin Campbell of the British army. The feud dated back many years when Joseph frowned upon his sister's marriage to Lord Curzon, and thus launched a long time battle with that British nobleman.

The dissatisfied heirs, among other things, questioned the settlement of the big wheat deal, asserting that the older Leiter had advanced nine million dol-

Joseph Leiter
*The Boy Plunger who played with millions at thirty was fighting
with royalty over other millions at sixty.*

lars, only two of which had been paid back in the intervening thirty years.

But the court's decision in the famous suit was an overwhelming victory for Joseph Leiter, who remained trustee of the big estate. In the decision he was pictured as a careful and industrious guardian of one of America's great fortunes, the funds entrusted to his care.

On the subject of the speculative catastrophe the court said:

"Counsel for complainant offered to show that Joseph Leiter spent approximately nine million dollars speculating in the wheat market and that his father paid his losses. While this court deemed the evidence incompetent, if admitted it would only tend to prove that Levi Z. Leiter knew that his son was of a speculative turn of mind—that he would take a chance—and with this knowledge, he made him his executor and trustee."

XVIII

A New Age

THE Pit still howls just as it howled in the stormy days of old when blustering pirates, riding the high seas of finance, ran terrorizing deals, rapped out orders that paralyzed the markets, and tipped over the laws of economics. Deep silence now pervades the dark pile of quaint architecture that blocks the foot of La Salle Street and seems to be in danger now of being swallowed up in a jungle of skyscrapers.

But the old days are gone, and with them the old practices that convulsed trade channels and upset the normal flow of commerce. Just as the towering personalities of Wall Street—the Uncle Dan'l Drews, the Deacon Whites, the Gates, and the Sages—have gone, leaving no counterparts, so the great plungers of the Wheat Pit have long since retired into the silences.

Men no longer stake immense fortunes on vast holdings and fight duels with money bags to the distress of legitimate business. No one man or group of men can bully and dictate and trample the trade marts with the sheer force of millions. To-day the machinery of speculation exists not for the few but for the many. And the transgressor at once becomes the enemy of all. Each trade is virtually an open record. The shout, the twinkling of finger signals, the nod, and the scrawl on the trading card, are all a part of the machinery constantly scrutinized for the slightest infraction.

Back in the dismal period following the civil war, a period of uncertainty and disillusionment, when thoughtful men wondered whether it had not all been in vain, there grew up the most bountiful crop of rugged speculators the nation has ever known. They were hard living, hard drinking men, reckless, and for the most part vain, greedy, and unscrupulous.

Wall Street's flame burned brightly, while markets were dragooned and plundered, while men rose to wealth and power both in the Wheat Pit and the Stock Exchange. The power of some seemed unlimited. They smashed precedent, changed rules to suit circumstances, and caused leaders of politics and society to bow down before them.

Curiously, in the end most of them met with disaster of one sort or another. A whirlwind would suddenly strike the man who had flown too high. His wealth would be swept away in a twinkling; his credit destroyed. His friends would desert him, and his name would become a by-word. Some of these human wrecks were little more than vagabonds, haunting the offices where they once held forth in splendor and, like ragged ghosts out of the past, pleading for one more chance.

In the case of the Wheat Pit, many strong men, calm and seemingly judicious, took up the task of cornering the market. Like a moth to a flame, each in turn would circle nearer and nearer, finally drawing close enough for ruin.

Indeed, nothing could be further from fact than the somewhat general impression that most of the old time wheat plungers were successful. Almost none of them made money in the Pit and kept it. Wall Street's plungers did little better.

"It is the speculator who is destroyed nine times out of ten," wrote Old Hutch in one of his last papers. "Look back fifty years. How many, as Jim Fisk said, have gone where the woodbine twineth?"

And flamboyant, melodramatic Jim Fisk knew what he was talking about. For he had himself helped to ruin a few of the outstanding plungers, as he went roaring through the teeming markets, breaking laws and bribing legislatures, a symbol of all that was bad in the worst days of stock speculation, a braggart who shouted defiantly: "There's no gallows built high enough to hang Jim Fisk!" And he did not wait for speculation to finish him, this man who shocked thick-skinned Wall Street by giving elaborate noon-time office parties to bevies of chorus girls, while the market boiled over. His was an even more dramatic ending; he died with a bullet in the belly, fired by a rival for the caresses of a scarlet lady.

Across the colorful pages of early speculative history Wall Street wrote misdeeds that would have put the Wheat Pit to shame. One gigantic outrage followed on the heels of another, each more flagrant than the last, each more stunning to the sensibilities of society.

A new dynamic idea was born in the world of commerce, when speculative markets finally felt and declared their wrongdoings. But in Wall Street, as in the Wheat Pit, years of blind groping, decades of serious, unbiased study were necessary to bring the stock and commodity exchanges up to their present high standard and forever to outlaw the pirates and adventurers who would blacken the name of competent speculation and hamper the nation's normal growth.

Slowly the evolution came about, step by step, a gain

here, a loss there, each constructive move meeting with opposition that was sometimes sincere and more often purely selfish.

A hundred different elements lay claim to the glory of bringing about the reform, the rebuilding of American exchanges. Some trace the inception of the movement way back to the seventies when the despised and inglorious Greenbackers, waving a flag of freedom for oppressed toilers, launched a fierce warfare upon the system of currency, the exchanges, and the railroads. They bitterly assailed corrupt politics, and not without justification, claiming that the holders of wealth controlled government and manipulated public affairs and markets to their own sweet advantage. No doubt this early cry in the wilderness was heard, for other upheavals followed that of the Greenbackers, who contented themselves by sending a few scowling, bewhiskered gents to Congress, to scare the sins out of the party bosses.

Later came the Populists with glittering promises to their followers and black threats for the big interests in politics and finance. This group was another bead strung upon the single strand of radicalism, and was even more clamorous in its outcries against the established order. But, like the Greenbackers, the Populists died of their own radicalism.

As the tides of public opinion rose and fell, other and lesser groups appeared. Politicians were forever taking up the war cry and, as usual, blocking the way to constructive reform. Being a creature of self-interest, with no deep convictions, the politician blundered along through the years, thoroughly muddling the issue. And yet history shows that some of those very ordinary self-seeking men, by reason of their zeal, became patriots and died with their admirers calling them statesmen.

Reformers and politicians and law makers did not cure the ills of speculation and correct the vicious practices born in the slumming days of the exchanges. Probably their outcries helped to point the way. But it was business and finance, big business if you like, prodded by public opinion, that finally cleaned up Wall Street and the commodity exchanges and the banking system and ushered in the new age of sane and regulated speculation.

The single powerful thought, expressed long before, the thought that honesty and integrity must prevail if ruin and decay were to be avoided, had at last crystalized into action. Like a bomb, that thought had been exploding over and over again for a period of thirty years.

In all the days of Wheat Pit reform, Old Hutch was pointed to as the emblem of destructive speculation. His dim figure, standing far back on the trail of time, was a specter used to call forth congressional shudders and the fearful chattering of political teeth.

As a consequence, many sins were unjustly laid at his door. Yet a close study of his life will fail to disclose a single act to which one might point and say: "Of that wrong you are guilty." Whatever his speculative indiscretions, he was bad only as, let us say, the doctors were bad in the days when they bled a patient to death in the belief that only drastic bleeding would save his life. They were doing what at the time seemed proper. So was Hutch. He never ran afoul of the law. And unlike many contemporaries, he never lent his genius to trickery, collusion, or deceit.

Opinion is somewhat divided in the matter of his value to society. A very few contend that he had no inborn love of justice and no beauty of character. They point to his intense dislike of social functions—a weak argument, indeed—to his neglect of home life during protracted campaigns in the Pit, to his relentless punishment of enemies.

There are far greater numbers, however, who direct attention to his splendid influence in the packing industry in the pioneering days, to his leadership in financial undertakings, such as banking and insurance, to his quick response with millions when the street or the city was in distress from panic. They assert he was a force that generated power and concentrated interest in the future of Chicago and the West and as such will some day receive his proper place in history.

Since no one ever pretended to thoroughly understand Old Hutch, and since those who knew him best had only quick glimpses of the real man during some fleeting moment, it is not surprising that diverse views should arise.

But all agree on the point that he distinctly represented an era in speculation, and that future historians will be inclined to carefully weigh his influence upon subsequent events, if only to determine whether he was the instrument through which all the weaknesses and blunders of a new and clumsy piece of commercial machinery were brought to light.

That he carried his deals beyond the line of common good there can be no doubt. But, as friends explained, his many failures in early life probably furnished the goad for him through some devilish inferiority complex which spurred him on to speculative excesses and dreams of immense power.

Certainly his life, so closely woven into the crazy pattern of nineteenth century speculation, demonstrated, for one thing, that corners are about the most ruinous luxury in which a speculator can indulge. Save for his one amazing success, by far the greatest of its kind in history, corners in breadstuffs, even in the most favorable days, were uniformly unsuccessful.

In the declining years of his life, Old Hutch rarely visited the scene of his many speculative wars. On occasion the desire to return to the conflict would flare up, and the old eagle would beat against his cage. But he knew full well he was unfitted for the Pit. Once or twice he was seen, a lonely figure, sitting in the public gallery, looking down with kindling eyes upon the four separate mobs rioting amid an incessant volume of outcries. And again he would be found reading the news on the tape: The monsoon in India was at hand. . . . Locusts had appeared in the Argentine. . . . The ice had gone out of the Danube. . . .

If his opinion were sought as to the future effect of some such report, he would shake his head slowly and say:

"Who is the man who can foretell events in this whirling, delirious world of fantasy?

"The longer I live, the more I am convinced of the wisdom of the quotation: 'Life is a song sung by an idiot, dancing down the wind!' "

When the chill of age was upon him, and he was spending his declining days in a sanitarium tucked deep in the wooded silences of Wisconsin, he would occasionally send for one of his old cronies, and together they would sit for hours musing and dreaming over the days that were dead. Or, again, they might ride for an afternoon in utter silence behind a team of spirited horses, groomed to the last extreme of shiny, satiny perfection.

But usually Old Hutch was alone and unsmiling in these drives, and in his long melancholy walks, and during hours of quiet meditation. More and more he complained that by leaving the Pit he had cut short his life and had likewise destroyed his only usefulness; that it was the throbbing Pit, with its joys and its agonies, that had stimulated his immense energies and had kept his mind burning with vivid dreams and lofty hopes.

Out of the Pit there was nothing. One empty day

crawled drearily into the next with neither victory nor defeat, for now there were no more battles to fight. Without the song of the Pit in his ears, time hung like a heavy weight. Of course Old Hutch loved good books, and so there was much reading to do, much verse to memorize, and there were speeches of famous statesmen to be analyzed and criticized. But in spite of all this playing at being busy, there were tortuous hours on end that were hollow and futile, hours that made old age cruelly dull to the man who had ridden so high. In those last lonely days Old Hutch might well have expressed his feelings in the words written by Mark Twain in the winter-time of his own life:

"Old age, white-headed, the temple empty, the idols broken, the worshipers in their graves; nothing but You, a remnant, a tradition, belated fag end of a foolish dream, a dream that was so ingeniously dreamed that it seemed real all the time; nothing left but You, center of a snowy desolation, perched on the ice-summit, gazing out over the stages of that long trek asking Yourself, 'Would you do it again if you had the chance?' "

He had made his last plunge and dreamed his last dream, and on March 16, 1899, the life of this restless old man with visions of world power came to a tranquil close. And they laid his tired body in the windowless house of peace.

(THE END.)

American Farmers
and
The Rise of Agribusiness

Seeds of Struggle

An Arno Press Collection

Allen, Ruth Alice. **The Labor of Women in the Production of Cotton.** 1933

Bailey, L[iberty] H[yde]. **Cyclopedia of American Agriculture.** Vol. II: Crops. 1912

Bankers and Beef. 1975

[Bivins, Frank Jarris]. **The Farmer's Political Economy.** 1913

Blumenthal, Walter Hart. **American Indians Dispossessed.** 1955

Brinton, J. W. **Wheat and Politics.** 1931

Caldwell, Erskine and Margaret Bourke-White. **You Have Seen Their Faces.** 1937

Cannery Captives. 1975

Children in the Fields. 1975

The Commission on Country Life. **Report of the Commission on Country Life.** 1911

The Co-operative Central Exchange. **The Co-operative Pyramid Builder.** three vols. July 1926-January 1931

Dies, Edward Jerome. **The Plunger:** A Tale of the Wheat Pit. 1929

Dunning, N. A. **The Farmers' Alliance History and Agricultural Digest.** 1891

Everitt, J[ames] A. **The Third Power:** Farmers to the Front. 1907

The Farmer-Labor Party—History, Platform and Programs. 1975

Greeley, Horace. **What I Know of Farming.** 1871

Hill, John, Jr. **Gold Bricks of Speculation.** 1904

Howe, Frederic C. **Privilege and Democracy in America.** 1910

James, Will. **Cowboys North and South.** 1924

Kerr, W[illiam] H[enry]. **Farmers' Union and Federation Advocate and Guide.** 1919

King, Clyde L. **Farm Relief.** 1929

Kinney, J. P. **A Continent Lost—A Civilization Won.** 1937

Land Speculation: New England's Old Problem. 1975

Lange, Dorothea and Paul Schuster Taylor. **An American Exodus:** A Record of Human Erosion. 1939

Lord, Russell. **Men of Earth.** 1931

Loucks, H[enry] L. **The Great Conspiracy of the House of Morgan and How to Defeat It.** 1916

Murphy, Jerre C. **The Comical History of Montana.** 1912

The National Nonpartisan League Debate. 1975

Orr, James L. **Grange Melodies.** 1911

Proctor, Thomas H. **The Banker's Dream.** 1895

Rochester, Anna. **Why Farmers Are Poor.** 1940

Russell, Charles Edward. **The Greatest Trust in the World.** 1905

Russell, Charles Edward. **The Story of the Nonpartisan League.** 1920

Simons, A. M. **The American Farmer.** 1902

Simonsen, Sigurd Jay. **The Brush Coyotes.** 1943

Todes, Charlotte. **Labor and Lumber.** 1931

U. S. Department of Labor. **Labor Unionism in American Agriculture.** 1945

U. S. Federal Trade Commission. **Cooperative Marketing.** 1928

U. S. Federal Trade Commission. **Report of the Federal Trade Commission on Agricultural Income Inquiry.** 1938. three vols. in two

U. S. Senate Committee on Education and Labor. **Violations of Free Speech and Rights of Labor.** 1941. three vols. in one

Vincent, Leopold. **The Alliance and Labor Songster.** 1891

Wallace, Henry C. **Our Debt and Duty to the Farmer.** 1925

Watson, Thomas E. **The People's Party Campaign Book.** [1893]

[White, Roland A.]. **Milo Reno, Farmers Union Pioneer.** 1941

Whitney, Caspar. **Hawaiian America.** 1899

Wiest, Edward. **Agricultural Organization in the United States.** 1923